TOUGH MINDED

SHANA ORCZYK SISSEL

TOUGH MINDED

HOW TAKING ON LIFE'S CHALLENGES CAN MAKE YOU A BETTER INVESTOR

WILEY

Published by John Wiley & Sons, Inc., Hoboken, New Jersey.

For general information on our other products and services or for technical support, please contact our Customer Care Department within the United States at (800) 762-2974, outside the United States at (317) 572-3993 or fax (317) 572-4002.

Wiley also publishes its books in a variety of electronic formats. Some content that appears in print may not be available in electronic formats. For more information about Wiley products, visit our web site at www.wiley.com.

Library of Congress Cataloging-in-Publication Data is Available:

ISBN 9781394386666 (Cloth)
ISBN 9781394386673 (ePub)
ISBN 9781394386680 (ePDF)

COVER DESIGN: PAUL MCCARTHY
COVER ART: LEYSANI/ADOBE STOCK PHOTOS

SKY10168224_091126

For Gabriel, who gave me every reason to keep going.

For Joe Alemany, who reminded me who I was.

And for Tina Powell, who showed all of us how to face the hardest chapter with grace, light, and unstoppable joy.

Contents

Foreword

By Robyn Murray[1]

Shana Sissel has survived not one but two terrorist attacks. On September 11, 2001, Sissel was on the 64th floor of World Trade Center Tower 2. On April 15, 2013, she was three blocks away from the finish line of the Boston Marathon.

Her frightening experiences, along with her childhood as the daughter of a police officer who shared his terrifying tales, have toughened her. And that toughness has given her an edge in her career—one where emotional decision making doesn't get you very far.

"Bullets in the junk drawer and evidence bags for lunches."

Shana Sissel grew up in Worcester, Massachusetts, a city about 40 miles west of Boston and considered a suburb of the bustling metropolis. She's a first-generation American—her mother was born and raised in Ireland; her father is Polish. She grew up painting *pisanki* (hard-boiled eggs) for Polish-themed Easters and watching the city turn green each spring in celebration of St. Patrick's Day. Her grandparents' siblings all lived within two blocks of each other, so her extended family was always around. "We were very family-oriented," Sissel recalled, "almost forcefully so."

---

[1] Murray, Robyn. (2018, December 5). "Tough Minded." CLS Investments. https://web.archive.org/web/20220923202613/https:/www.clsinvest.com/2018/12/05/tough-minded/

Sissel's father was a police officer in Worcester, an area with substantial crime, which often made his job dangerous. "My father was involved in all kinds of shootings," she said. "He had lots of crazy cop stories." As a kid, she didn't hear the worst ones. But as she has gotten older, he has filled in some gruesome details (one often-told tale involves a decapitated head). Sissel says she finds it hard to explain what growing up as a "cop kid" was like because that's all she has ever known. "It's cool when you're eight and your dad takes you to school in the cruiser with the sirens on. And of course, it makes dating interesting when your dad shows up in uniform with a gun." Other than that, she sums it up this way: "We always had bullets in the junk drawer, and my mom used evidence bags for lunches."

Sissel's mother was an inner-city school teacher, and she says her parents urged her to find a similar blue-collar career, one with the safety of a union and a pension. "But that just wasn't me," she said. "My family all says I'm a different animal."

When Sissel thought about what she wanted for her future, she thought of her uncle, Stan. He was a self-made man who worked his way up to owning an oil company and becoming very wealthy. She remembers being impressed as a child that he drove a Mercedes-Benz and handed out generous checks for Christmas. "My grandmother idolized him," she said. "When he was coming to visit from New York, everything had to look perfect."

Sissel saved a newspaper article about her uncle's oil company and imagined herself leading the kind of life where something like that was possible. "It wasn't that I dreamed of being rich. Uncle Stan just seemed to be really important, and I wanted to be really important one day."

After receiving her bachelor's degree in sports management, Sissel began considering a career in finance. She called her uncle for advice, and he told her to go for it. So, in May 2001 Sissel took the first step with a position at Morgan Stanley as a financial advisor.

She loved it. "I loved learning about the markets, listening to the analysts, and just being part of the glamorous world of finance," she said.

On September 11, 2001, Sissel was working at Morgan Stanley at 2 World Trade Center when terrorists hijacked two planes and careened them into the Twin Towers. She says she and the other 2,500 employees owe their lives to the chief of security at Morgan Stanley, Rick Rescorla, who evacuated the building as soon as the first plane hit Tower 1, ignoring orders by the Port Authority to remain. Even as the building shook and went dark after the second plane hit, Rescorla kept the employees moving down the stairs, singing war-time battle songs to keep their spirits up. Morgan Stanley lost six employees that day. Rescorla was one of them. He went back in to the building to make sure everyone was out, and that's when it collapsed.

Sissel was shaken by the experience. For the next few months, she was in limbo while the firm figured out how to get everyone back to work. She used the time to learn about building portfolios, research stocks and mutual funds, read about the markets, and recover from the trauma of what had happened.

"I certainly don't have rose-colored glasses."

Two years later, Sissel took another step in furthering her financial career by enrolling in an MBA program at Bentley University. In 2004, she was hired at Fidelity Investments as an internal wholesaler and investment analyst. Three years later, she moved to Seattle for a position as an equity portfolio analyst with Russell Investments, and in 2008, she moved back to Boston to join Peak Financial Management as a research analyst and investment strategist.

It was there that Sissel discovered perhaps one of her favorite aspects of working in finance: talking about it. At Peak, she became the go-to source for numerous financial publications. She was interviewed by the *Wall Street Journal* and the *Financial Times*. She was a regular on local news programs in Boston and was featured on CNBC. She loved it, and she excelled at it. "I like to be the center of attention," she said, "and that really played into that aspect of my personality."

The founder of Peak later retired, and Sissel moved on to Mercer and then returned to Fidelity as a fundamental research analyst for Strategic Advisers. She was responsible for identifying investment disciplines and recommending managers to execute them, and she felt like she'd come full circle in her career.

Then, another terrorist attack jolted her world. On April 15, 2013, Sissel was three blocks from the finish line of the Boston Marathon when two homemade pressure cooker bombs exploded, killing three people and injuring hundreds.

Similar to the fog of 9/11, the days following the bombing were a haze of trauma and grief in Boston, exacerbated by the manhunt to track the bombers. Sissel's family was intimately involved. Her sister is a 911 dispatcher, so she told Sissel about the shelter-in-place order before most had heard it, and her brother-in-law is the head of SWAT for the Worcester Police Department, so he provided backup for the Boston police and FBI as they tracked the bombers. It was a shared trauma that united the city of Boston. "My instinct was to help the people around me prepare and deal with the emotional toll of the experience," Sissel said. "In a weird way I was really proud to be in Boston through all that."

The experiences of growing up hearing about violence and danger and then living through two of the worst attacks on U.S. soil have shaped the way Sissel views the world. "I've gotten very close to stuff that is very distant to a lot of people," she said. "I certainly don't have rose-colored glasses, and I think I have a healthy level of paranoia."

They've also hardened her to a degree, which, luckily, is a valuable quality as an investor. "I've been through emotionally traumatic things. And that means—as an investor—other people's emotions don't influence me as much."

Sissel is also resilient. And tough. As a professional, she is unafraid to play devil's advocate in meetings and push people to see the other side. She's curious and always looking for more information—even when it proves her wrong, sometimes particularly so.

In fact, she's just the kind of person that CLS Chief Investment Officer Rusty Vanneman would want to work with. Vanneman and Sissel have a mentor in common: Art Lutschaunig, the founder of Fidelity Strategic Advisers. That's what prompted Sissel to look up Vanneman after she moved to Chicago with her husband and now 3-year-old son to be closer to her husband's family.

"Art has a certain kind of person that he hires that does well," Sissel said. "People that don't keep their opinions to themselves and are not afraid to take risks or think outside the box. Rusty is that kind of person, and so am I." Sissel applied for a remote position at CLS and came on board as a portfolio manager in September 2018.

While it has been a winding road to get here, with more than enough challenges to overcome, the journey has made Sissel an asset as an investment manager, and she will no doubt make her mark at CLS. As she describes "Art's people," "We're tough. And that makes me good at what I do."

Preface

Over the past two decades, many people have told me, "You should write a book," after hearing my story. While I've always appreciated the compliment, I never quite saw myself as worthy of a spot on someone's bookshelf. Call it imposter syndrome, but in my mind, I'm just a girl from a blue-collar, immigrant family in Worcester, Massachusetts. We don't seek fame or acclaim; we just put our heads down and do the work. No fanfare, just good old-fashioned work ethic.

But I've never been one to shy away from the spotlight. The more I was encouraged, the more I wondered if writing a book might actually be possible.

As you'll discover through each chapter, my life has never been boring. Nothing about my upbringing is particularly unique, but how I've grown out of it might be the part that resonates with you. The lessons I've learned through many hardships have been profound and have shaped who I am today. Most notably, they've fueled my success as an investor.

The title of this book isn't something I can claim credit for, nor is the core idea. In 2018, I joined a firm then called CLS Investments. CLS was an investment management firm embedded within a larger financial technology company called Orion Advisor Technology. At the time, Orion was a well-known leader in the world of independent investment advisors—providing top-tier back-office technology solutions.

When I joined CLS, my role was to work with a team developing an optimization tool for customizing direct index solutions. The team was young, was passionate, and, like me, grew up in a somewhat unconventional environment. One of our traditions was to introduce new members through a spotlight blog post, helping clients and colleagues get to know us better. That post was written by a talented freelance writer named Robyn Murray.

The process was simple: Robyn would interview you and then craft her piece with the creativity and flair that only a professional copywriter and editor can bring. The piece she wrote about me was called "Tough Minded," and the way she captured my story in that short blog blew me away.

That spotlight post inspired this book. So, with Robyn's permission, I want to share it with you now. Since she wrote those words, I've faced even more challenges, but her reflection remains an inspiring way to set the tone for what's to come.

What you're about to read is a blend of personal memoir and investment strategy—two worlds that have deeply shaped my life. While I still question whether my story is truly worthy of a book, I hope that as you read, you'll find both inspiration and insight into the world of investing—a world that has become my life's passion.

Acknowledgments

A book is never written alone, and this one is no exception. To my family: my parents, my brother Neal, and my sisters Kerri and Chrissy—thank you for being the foundation everything else was built on. You showed me what it means to work hard, love fiercely, and refuse to quit. And to my son Gabriel: you are the reason for all of it. Every hard chapter, every time I got back up, every day I chose to keep going—it was for you. Watching you become the person you are is the greatest privilege of my life.

To my ride-or-die crew—John Fonseca, Shawna Ohm, Brittany Mason, and Allison Stockwell—there are no words adequate to what you gave me during the hardest years of my life. You showed up without being asked, you stayed without being told to, and you held me together when I could not hold myself. I would not be here without you. I mean that in every sense.

To the mentors who saw something in me worth investing in—Tom Allen, Sue Thompson, Art Lutschaunig, Rusty Vanneman, Daniel Bryant, Jamie Hopkins, and Tyrone Ross—thank you for your guidance, your honesty, and your willingness to open doors and tell me the truth in equal measure. The best advice I ever received came from this group, and the fingerprints of those conversations are on every page of this book.

Finally, to the investors who continue to inspire the way I think about markets and what is possible within them—Cliff Asness, Matt Hougan, and Vincent Sellecchia—thank you for setting a standard of intellectual rigor and independent conviction that I have spent my career trying to live up to.

About the Author

Shana Orczyk Sissel is the founder and CEO of Banríon Capital Management and one of the financial industry's most recognized voices on alternative investing. Known as the Queen of Alternatives, she has spent more than two decades championing broader access to investment strategies once reserved exclusively for institutions and the ultra-wealthy—building a career that spans some of the most consequential moments in modern market history.

A sought-after speaker, media contributor, and thought leader, Shana has appeared regularly on Fox Business, CNBC, and Bloomberg, and has been featured in leading financial publications throughout her career. Her firm, Banríon Capital Management, was recognized as a WealthTech 100 Company of 2026 by FinTech Global.

Tough Minded is her first book—part investing guide, part memoir, and entirely her own story. It is the account of a woman who learned everything she knows about markets from the life she actually lived: the losses, the reinventions, the moments of crisis that turned out to be the education no classroom could have provided. It is written for anyone who has ever felt like the room wasn't built for them—and decided to walk in anyway.

Shana lives in the Chicago area with her son Gabriel. She is currently in treatment for stage IV metastatic breast cancer and has no intention of slowing down.

Chapter 1

Foundations of Resilience: The Immigrant Mindset and Heritage

First-Generation American

"*Chodź tutaj!*" I can still hear my grandmother's stern voice, requesting "come here" in Polish. Growing up in a multilingual household is truly a special experience. Polish culture was infused into my life from the moment I was born. I vividly remember our daily walks down Water Street to Widoff's Bakery, where I'd shop for the freshest Eastern European pastries. I can still taste the raspberry *kołaczki*, dusted with extra powdered sugar, of course. Every fall, I eagerly looked forward to apple picking, knowing that *racuchy z jablkami* (apple pancakes) would be on the breakfast menu the next morning. I've mastered my grandmother's recipe and still love spending a Sunday morning making them each autumn.

According to the U.S. Census Bureau, there are approximately 23 million first-generation Americans as of 2023. I am one of them. My mother was born in County Kerry, Ireland, in a family rooted in large Irish clans of laborers and clergy. It was an intriguing mix—bricklayers, farmers, nuns, and priests. However, my maternal grandfather, Cornelius, chose a different path—he pursued opportunities in hospitality.

An Irish Heritage

It made sense; he was a gregarious man, known for his love of socializing and a good drink. In Killarney, Ireland, opportunities in hospitality were abundant. My grandfather worked as a porter at high-end hotels in the tourist area of Killarney, while my grandmother, Kathleen, an accomplished Irish dancer, taught her three children the art of Irish dance to help make ends meet. She even made their costumes from curtains.

The three children, already blessed with the coveted tight curls of the Irish dancing aesthetic, often entertained tourists in the evenings at a local hotel in Killarney. Life in Ireland was tough, and my grandfather sought a better future for his family.

My grandmother's brother, Timothy, had emigrated to the United States in 1925. He had served as a member of the Irish Republican Army's intelligence division from 1916 until the Irish Civil War ended in 1924. During his service, he was a war hero—imprisoned by the British in 1922 and spending 13 days on a hunger strike. In 1952, he was awarded a bronze medal by the President of Ireland in recognition of his bravery.

Uncle Timmy became a notable figure in Worcester, Massachusetts, serving in leadership roles for the Worcester Housing Authority, the Worcester City Council, and the local Knights of Columbus. A skilled contractor with a laborer's heart, he sponsored my mother's family when they immigrated to the United States. My mom was just nine years old when she arrived—a tough, fearless kid, eager to fit into a culture so different from her own. She got into her share of trouble in her youth, trying to find her place.

Both my grandparents worked in hospitality—my grandfather as a server and doorman, my grandmother as a maid. They arrived in America with very little money, and life was anything but easy.

Bridging Two Worlds

My father's family shares that same immigrant story, but from a different region. My paternal grandparents were Polish. My grandmother fled Poland as World War I broke out. My grandfather was born in the United States, although his mother returned to Poland shortly after his birth. He spent his early years living with her and her family before returning to the United States as the war reached Poland.

Both my paternal grandparents were multilingual: my grandfather spoke English, Polish, Russian, Lithuanian, and French, while my grandmother spoke English, Polish, and Russian. They mostly communicated with us in Polish and argued in Russian. To this day, I can still recognize the distinct sounds of Russian, Polish, Lithuanian, and Czech—though my ability to speak Polish fluently has long since faded.

My paternal grandparents were the oldest children in their large families, while my maternal grandparents were the youngest. My maternal grandparents faced the challenges that come with a significant sibling age gap—more than 25 years—and a family that spread across several countries. In contrast, my paternal grandparents maintained close ties with their siblings, all of whom lived in the ethnic Eastern European neighborhoods of Vernon Hill and Grafton Hill in Worcester.

Meanwhile, my mother's family mostly remained in Ireland. Unlike my paternal side, which kept strong connections with each other living in the same neighborhood, my mother's family stayed an ocean away. My maternal grandfather died just months before I was born, and shortly after my first birthday, my maternal grandmother moved back to Ireland.

My mother's immigrant roots helped her fit in with my father's family. There was a shared experience across the group, and while my paternal grandfather would playfully call her a "Harp" on occasion, she quickly embraced Polish traditions. She even worked as a teacher at a Catholic school associated with Our Lady of Czestochowa Parish, a school that emphasized speaking Polish and was largely run by nuns of Polish descent.

The American Dream: A Land of Opportunity

Growing up among immigrants is a unique experience. When families choose to come to the United States to escape extreme poverty, war, and communism, their view of American culture is often idealistic. They've endured hardships that only other immigrants can truly understand, and they see America as the land of opportunity. They don't consider low-skill, low-wage jobs beneath them—rather, they view these positions as necessary steps to give their children a better life.

My paternal grandfather, Stanley, worked in a steel mill, while my paternal grandmother, Anna, worked on the assembly line at a company that made roller skates during World War II and for many years afterward. She worked the day shift, and he worked the night shift, so my father spent more time with my grandfather as a child. Their marriage was arranged by their fathers, who were drinking buddies at the local White Eagle Club. They raised three boys: my Uncle Stan was born shortly after they married but remained an only child for the first 13 years of his life—the economic challenges of the Great Depression made having more children difficult. My Uncle Ronnie was born in 1943, followed by my father shortly after the end of World War II. With two working parents, my dad was often shuffled off to the homes of relatives, where close family bonds were reinforced and deeply ingrained in our family dynamic.

Growing up, I believed I had a huge extended family—both my parents insisted we call their cousins by "Aunt" or "Uncle," reflecting a bond that felt almost like siblings. Family traditions centered on our old culture: we spoke Polish, celebrated Polish Easter and Christmas, and marked St. Patrick's Day with Irish customs.

Lessons from My Parents: Work Ethic and Resilience

Both my parents worked as civil servants—my mom as a teacher and my dad as a police officer. My dad was influenced by his uncles. My grandfathers' two sisters, my Great Aunt Sophie and my Great Aunt Helen, married men in law enforcement.

All three Orczyk brothers served in the military: my dad, eager to enlist, did so at 17 with his parents' written permission. My Uncle Stan served as a Marine during the Korean War and received a Bronze Star. My Uncle Ronnie served as a sergeant in the Air Force, stationed in Germany for most of his enlistment. My dad was a Navy corpsman in Vietnam. His military experience was brutal, but he thrived within the structure it provided. His uncles encouraged him to join the police force, valuing the discipline and order it offered.

My dad was a proud police officer; my mom, on the other hand, was a proud troublemaker—fiery, outspoken, and resilient.

Growing up in a family where women worked and men actively participated in raising children, it's no surprise my father was drawn to a woman like my mom—strong, independent, and unafraid to speak her mind. He instilled in his children to be self-reliant, to be resilient, and to develop a strong work ethic.

Because of my dad's profession, we were often exposed to the darker threads of human nature. We saw the worst of human behavior on a regular basis. As a child, I reflected my parents' contrasting personalities: the tough, no-nonsense, do-it-yourself attitude of my dad, combined with my mom's spirited, feisty, confrontational nature. I was never afraid to speak my mind, even if it got me in trouble, and I never backed down from a fight. I was acutely aware of the underbelly of human nature, with a healthy dose of paranoia ingrained in me.

My dad made sure his daughters knew they were capable of anything. There were no limits based on gender—yet he also wanted us to be ladies, with good manners and always presentable. This internal struggle—balancing femininity with toughness—was a challenge I wrestled with. I loved makeup and dresses, but I also played soccer and earned the nickname "The Terminator" for my aggressive, often rough play—once even getting suspended from school for punching a boy on the bus who tried to kiss me.

Finding My Place: Finance and the Immigrant Mindset

It's no surprise, then, that I chose a career in the male-dominated industry of finance. My upbringing suited me perfectly for an environment filled with power-hungry men. I've never been bothered by locker room talk, discussing last night's game, or being the only woman in the room. Instead, I challenge the status quo.

The greatest advantage my upbringing has given me is that I'm not easily intimidated. Additionally, as an investor, viewing the world through an immigrant mindset is incredibly valuable. It has enabled me to identify potential opportunities that can lead to successful investments, while also being acutely aware of the risks—what might go horribly wrong. That healthy paranoia stems from growing up as the daughter of a cop, and it's a crucial trait in investing.

In fact, I'd argue that understanding the bear case of an investment is often more valuable than seeing only the bullish potential. The willingness to consider viewpoints different from your own—whether they come from a different approach or a different experience—helps you see beyond your bubble, engage in healthy debate, and maintain an open mind. This mental flexibility is critical for success as an investor.

You must be willing to consider all potential outcomes, to cut through the noise of the crowd and your personal biases. That's the foundation for making sound investment decisions. Financial markets are largely driven by groupthink and personal bias. Being contrarian and considering diverse strategies gives you a real edge as an investor.

The Power of Perspective

My hope with this book is to offer you a relatable and approachable perspective on investing. It's not just about the math or the complexities of financial markets—it's about understanding what truly makes someone a good investor. The most successful investors I've met don't owe their success to being the smartest mathematicians or having Nobel Prize–winning economics degrees. Take Peter Lynch, for example. What made him exceptional was his genuine curiosity—his willingness to talk to people, ask insightful questions, and truly grasp the businesses he was investing in. Will Danoff often found his best ideas by observing the trends that excited his kids or by uncovering subtle insights during earnings calls about the competitive landscape.

Malcolm Gladwell's book, *Blink*, delves into the idea of the adaptive unconscious—the notion that our past experiences, memories, and dreams help us make quick decisions in the blink of an eye, often without us even realizing it. Whether you call it intuition or instinct, what it boils down to is that our life stories and experiences shape our behavior and our gut reactions.

What truly makes someone a good investor isn't necessarily academic achievement, but the wealth of their life experiences that influence their worldview. This, I believe, becomes their superpower. My hope is that by sharing what has shaped my own, you'll be inspired to discover and cultivate your unique superpower too.

Chapter 2

Roots of Hard Work: Blue-Collar Values and Risk Management

Saturday Nights and Survival Economics

It's a Saturday night, and my brother and I are sitting at the kitchen table, waiting for my mom to pull the Monopoly board out of the hall closet. Saturday nights were always family game night when I was growing up. They were sacred.

Once a month, my dad actually joined us. That alone made it special. Most Saturdays, he was working a pay job, whatever he could find to bring in extra income for our family. Those jobs ranged from working the door at El Morocco, the legendary Lebanese restaurant and jazz club in Worcester, Massachusetts, to providing security at iconic nightlife spots like Maxwell Silverman's. Sometimes he worked security for high-profile entertainers performing at the Centrum (now the DCU Center). On rare occasions, it was a seedy strip club that needed help handling rowdy patrons. To a kid, it all felt glamorous, rubbing elbows with the rich and famous, hearing stories about celebrities, and watching my dad move comfortably in spaces that felt larger than life.

He was the officer of preference for many of the families who owned these establishments, and that came with perks. For most of my childhood, I genuinely believed Arnie Ravelson, the patriarch behind the legendary "Maurice the Pants Man," was my uncle. He always took care of us. Red Sox tickets at Fenway. A new Starter jacket at Christmas. When I was 10, I wanted to buy Christmas presents for my family. Uncle Arnie let me sort hangers in the stockroom on Saturday afternoons so I could earn some money and get the employee discount. It was my first lesson in work equaling opportunity.

Working Parents, Shared Sacrifice

We were not a wealthy family. My parents worked constantly just to make sure the bills were paid.

Before I was born, my mom had been a kindergarten teacher in the Worcester Public Schools. She loved teaching and was good at it, but she left her career to become a stay-at-home mom. It didn't take long for them to realize that no amount of pay jobs could make a single income work. So, my mom did what she had to do; she went back to work.

To make childcare possible, my parents worked opposite hours. One of the more memorable jobs my mom took was as a nightshift beat reporter for the *Worcester Telegram & Gazette*, at that time still being published as the *Morning Telegram and the Evening Gazette*. She'd leave for work right around my bedtime, and I hated it. I showed my displeasure by ripping pages out of my books and throwing them at the door.

When my brother was born a few years later, things became even harder. Supporting a family of four, plus child support and alimony for my dad's two older daughters from his first marriage, required my mom to take higher-paying roles, including a job as a loan officer at WCIS Bank. At that point, my grandparents stepped in, watching my brother and me most days, and often nights too. It wasn't glamorous. But it was stable. And stability mattered.

Work Ethic as a Requirement, Not a Choice

Work ethic wasn't taught in my family; it was modeled daily. As soon as I was old enough, my dad required me to get a job. If I wanted to participate in activities, I paid for them myself. Horseback riding. Skiing. Beauty pageants. All on me.

My dad saw scholarship potential in soccer, and eventually that consumed my life. Even then, I worked whenever I could on off-days. No job was ever beneath me. Work was simply what you did to support the life you wanted. That belief has never left me.

The Household Finance Meeting

Once a month, before the games came out of the closet, my parents sat down at the dining room table for their "household finance meeting." At the time, I didn't understand how unusual this was.

I was never formally included, but I began finding reasons to linger. At first, I was just a kid waiting for the adults to finish so we could get to the good part of the weekend. But somewhere along the way, the waiting became watching, and the watching became something else entirely. The ritual of it caught my attention—the seriousness with which my parents approached the table, the language they used, the way decisions were made out loud and together. By the time I was old enough to understand what I was observing, I was already hooked.

My dad sat at the head of the table with a stack of bills. My mom sat beside him with the bank statements and the checkbook. Together, they reviewed every line item. Every bill. Every obligation. They separated expenses by priority and calculated exactly how much income was required to keep a roof over our heads and the cars running. Then they talked about goals. A family vacation. Summer camp for the kids. And then came the hard part: figuring out how many extra hours they would need to work to afford those things.

Some things were non-negotiable. Weekly date nights mattered. Family game night mattered. Sometimes that meant my dad picked up a late-night pay job, usually the strip club gig, that his partner usually covered. It was not his favorite; it meant prioritizing the money earned over sleep. Dealing with the darker side of life, the side that made you take an extra shower when you got home, sometimes was essential. It was just enough to close the gap in the budget, while still protecting the time that mattered most. Looking back, it was risk management in its purest form.

Every decision balanced risk and return. The risks were burnout, health, strained relationships, and financial instability. The returns were a strong marriage, grounded children, and long-term household stability. They weren't trying to build wealth. They were trying to survive. That realization came much later.

How This Shaped My Relationship with Money

As an adult, I've come to understand just how deeply this ritual shaped my approach to money. I've always been rigid with budgeting and risk management. That rigidity protected me in many ways, but it also created challenges. My ex-husband and I did not share financial values, and that mismatch led to constant stress and, ultimately, financial implosion. What I carried forward from my parents—the need for structure, predictability, and security—clashed with a very different philosophy.

What never changed was my willingness to work. I have never been afraid of effort. I have always lived by my dad's core rule: make sure there's a roof over your head, food on the table, and a reliable way to get where you need to go.

The Lesson That Matters Most

This may be the most important lesson in this book: *money needs to be talked about.* Openly, honestly, and without shame. Risk and return should be evaluated continuously. Stability should be prioritized before but not at the expense of building wealth. Most importantly, your relationship with money is rarely about numbers alone; it's about survival, safety, and the stories you absorbed as a child.

Learning how to build wealth required me to actively challenge the rigidity that once kept me safe. It required new skills: scenario planning, earnings reviews, cash-flow analysis, and trusted partners who could help me see beyond my base case.

Starting the Conversation

Most people don't lack the desire to have honest conversations about money. They lack a door in. The subject carries so much accumulated silence: inherited shame, unspoken fear, the sense that talking about it openly is somehow indiscreet or unseemly, that even people who love each other deeply can go years, or entire lifetimes, without once having a genuine exchange about how they actually think about financial security, risk, or what they want their money to make possible. My parents didn't wait for the perfect moment or the right language. They sat down at the dining room table once a month and did the work together. That simple act of consistency did more to shape my financial thinking than any course or credential ever could. If you don't have a version of that in your life yet, here is how to begin building one:

- *With a partner or spouse:* The most effective entry point is not a budget spreadsheet; it's a question about history. Ask your partner what money felt like when they were growing up. Was it a source of stress or security? Was it discussed openly or treated as a subject that lived behind closed doors? Those early experiences are the invisible architecture beneath every financial disagreement a couple will ever have. Understanding where each of you started makes it possible to build something intentional together, rather than simply colliding over the residue of two different childhoods. Once you have had that conversation, the practical one, about income, expenses, goals, and what you are each willing to sacrifice for what, becomes significantly easier to navigate.

- *With aging parents:* This is the conversation most adult children postpone indefinitely, and the one they most regret not having sooner. You don't have to begin with estate planning or account numbers. You can begin with curiosity: ask your parents about the financial decisions they made that they are proud of and the ones they would approach differently. Ask what they wish someone had told them earlier. Ask what they want their later years to look like and what they need to feel secure. These questions open the door without demanding anything, and they tend to surface the practical information, the accounts, the documents, the plans, naturally over time. The goal of the first conversation is not to solve everything. It is simply to establish that this is a subject your family can discuss without shame.
- *With your children:* You do not need to wait until they are old enough to understand compound interest. My first financial education happened at a kitchen table, watching my parents take the subject seriously. Children absorb the emotional register of money long before they understand the mechanics. If they see you approach it with calm, with structure, with the sense that this is a normal and important part of adult life, that is what they will carry forward. Let them see you make a budget. Explain, in age-appropriate terms, why you are choosing one thing over another. Give them small financial decisions to practice with and let them experience the consequences of both good choices and poor ones. The goal is not to burden them with adult anxieties. It is to make financial thinking feel natural, manageable, and fundamentally normal.

- *With yourself:* Before any of these conversations can be fully honest, this one has to happen first. Sit down, without a phone, without distraction, and write down what money has meant to you at each stage of your life. What did you believe about it as a child? What do you believe about it now? Where do those beliefs serve you, and where do they hold you back? What are you afraid to look at directly? The household finance meeting my parents held every month was not just about numbers. It was an act of radical honesty between two people committed to facing reality together. You cannot invite anyone else into that kind of honesty until you have practiced it with yourself first.

The conversation doesn't have to be formal. It doesn't require a spreadsheet or a financial planner or the right time. It just requires someone willing to go first. In most families, most relationships, most households, that person has never existed. It can be you. It should be you. The discomfort of starting that conversation is far smaller than the cost of never having it.

Your Turn: Reflecting on the Roots

I challenge you to reflect on your own relationship with money. What was your version of the household finance meeting? Did you have one at all? What moments from your formative years shaped how you view risk, work, and security? What needs healing? And as you reflect, ask yourself one more question: who is watching you now? Because whether we realize it or not, we are always teaching someone how to think about money, work, and worth. Our financial habits are formed early, but they are not fixed. Change begins with awareness, honesty, and a work ethic that aligns with the life we are trying to build.

From Survival to Strategy

The environment I grew up in trained me to think about money as something fragile. Something that could disappear if you weren't vigilant. That mindset is not wrong. In fact, it is foundational. But survival thinking and wealth-building thinking are not the same.

My parents practiced risk management long before I ever knew the term. They stress-tested income. They prioritized fixed obligations. They protected what mattered most. What they didn't do, and what they couldn't afford to do, was take *asymmetric risk* in pursuit of long-term upside. As an investor and business builder, I had to learn how to expand beyond survival without abandoning discipline.

That tension—between protection and growth—is at the heart of every investment decision. Later in this book, I talk about sexier topics like portfolio management, hedge funds, private equity, and the path to money management for the wealthy. But all of those concepts rest on something much deeper: your emotional relationship with money.

- If your foundation is rooted in fear, you will underinvest.
- If your foundation is rooted in fantasy, you will overreach.
- If your foundation is rooted in clarity, you can do both: protect and grow.

This chapter has explained why my investing philosophy begins with risk awareness, cash flow visibility, and honest conversations, not returns. You cannot build intelligently on top of a shaky emotional base. Before we move forward into strategy, we pause here—because this is where everything starts.

Your relationship with money did not begin with your first paycheck or your first investment account. It began much earlier—through observation, necessity, and survival. To change your financial future, you don't need to reject that history. You need to understand it. Only then can discipline evolve into strategy, and effort evolve into intention.

Chapter 3

The Rule Follower and the Rule Breaker: Navigating Contrasts, Cultivating Identity, and Balancing Strength with Grace

"Once You Meet My Parents, I Make Sense"

Before I introduce anyone to my parents, I always say the same thing: "Once you meet my parents, I make a lot more sense." It's true. My parents could not be more different if they tried. Their personalities are a living embodiment of the phrase opposites attract. And yet, they've been married for nearly five decades. What they share is what actually matters: values, work ethic, resilience, and an immigrant mindset shaped by poverty, hardship, and a deep belief that family comes first.

Of all their children, I am almost certainly the one who most reflects the tension, and the synthesis, of their contrasting approaches to life.

My Father: The Rule Follower, The Protector

My dad is a tough guy. An alpha male from a long line of alpha men. These were men who believed it was their duty to provide, protect, and lead. Men who measured worth through responsibility and endurance. That sense of duty didn't stop at fatherhood; it extended fully into his role as a husband.

Despite his exterior, my dad is a hopeless romantic. Roses "just because." An insistence that his wife shouldn't have to do anything physically taxing. Affectionate to the point that his children cringed watching their parents cuddle. As a teenager, it was *ewwwww*. As an adult watching them behave the exact same way in their 70s, it's more like #goals.

He joined the military at 17, like his father before him. His brothers, cousins, and uncles all enlisted as soon as they were able. He served as a corpsman in Vietnam, returned home, worked in a morgue, and saw the darkest side of life early and often. Law enforcement was a natural calling. The structure suited him. The rules made sense. The threat assessment became instinct.

To meet my dad is to feel evaluated. He reads people instantly. He scans environments automatically. He is physically imposing and deeply intimidating without saying a word. Everything about him communicates order, discipline, and boundaries. That presence was intentional.

My paternal grandfather, 5′7″ on a good day, built his body so he could fully embody the protector archetype. A national powerlifting champion with the Polish American Federation, he turned physical strength into armor. My dad followed suit, starting in the weight room in high school and turning strength into competition and then into identity. Massive chest. Thick neck. Unreal forearms. No nonsense. No ambiguity.

My Mother: The Rule Breaker, The Challenger

My mom, on the other hand, is a rebel. She's feisty. Sharp. She is what we lovingly call in New England a smart ass. She has a temper, a short fuse, and absolutely no interest in blindly following rules. She is the life of the party and the troublemaker in the room.

She would have been miserable in the military. Independent. Defiant. Unafraid of confrontation. As a public-school teacher in the inner city, these traits made her exceptional. She connected with her students because she spoke their language. Nothing shocked her. No one intimidated her. She knew exactly how to handle the difficult kid, and she never hesitated to challenge authority when it mattered. Administration didn't always love her. But her students did.

Her legendary stories include beating up the mayor's daughter for mocking her and pushing a nun down a dumbwaiter to avoid getting caught smoking in the bathroom. She will absolutely cause a scene if a clerk is condescending or mistreats a co-worker. She chooses confrontation when it's warranted.

Her first interaction with my dad? Informing him she wasn't falling for his pickup lines and the uniform didn't work on her.

The Attraction: Strength Meets Defiance

My dad was drawn to my mom because she wasn't impressed or intimidated by him. She didn't need him. She didn't follow his rules. And at a time when women like that were rare, that spirit captivated him.

Their relationship has never been dull. The spark lives in that tension. The balance between structure and rebellion, discipline and defiance. It's why my dad ultimately embraced the strong-woman archetype. It's why all of his daughters have "attitudes."

And it's why the relationships I seek mirror theirs. I seek strength and resilience. Assertiveness and wit. Femininity paired with toughness. Strong men who embody the provider-protector archetype, alongside my own independence and self-sufficiency. That duality is not accidental. It was modeled.

Growing up inside this contrast taught me something most people struggle to learn:

- You can respect the rules without becoming constrained by them.
- You can challenge authority without becoming reckless.
- You can operate inside systems while refusing to be defined by them.

This is where my edge comes from. Financially and otherwise.

Where Most People Fail

This duality is critical to success in investing. Rule breakers fail because they believe rules don't apply to them. They ignore structure, underestimate risk, and eventually self-destruct. Rule followers fail because they follow the crowd. They fear standing apart. They confuse compliance with safety and miss opportunity as a result.

The most successful investors live in the gray area. They understand the rules deeply and then they think independently within them. They respect constraints but they don't outsource judgment. They push boundaries without crossing lines that end careers or capital. That balance: structure plus creativity, discipline plus intuition, is rare. And it is learnable.

John Paulson's short against the housing market in 2006 is the archetype. He didn't reject the rules of the mortgage market; he mastered them so completely that he saw what participants operating purely on consensus had stopped looking for. The conviction was contrarian. The execution was disciplined. Neither alone produces that outcome. But together, they allowed him to execute one of the most legendary trades in financial history.

Your Turn: Know Yourself Before You Know the Market

When you are in a room full of people who believe something you don't, what do you do? Do you voice the disagreement or let it go because the social cost feels too high? When someone in authority tells you something with confidence, do you accept it or probe it? When the people closest to you push back on a decision you've made, do you reconsider genuinely—or just perform consideration before holding the line? These are not abstract personality questions. They are the foundation of every investment decision you will ever make. The investor who can't sit comfortably in disagreement will always be late. The one who reflexively defies consensus will confuse stubbornness for conviction. Neither instinct, unchecked, builds wealth. Your tendencies were formed long before you ever thought about markets—in what you were rewarded for, what you were penalized for, and what you watched the adults around you do under pressure. The best investors are not fearless. They are self-aware. That awareness isn't something the market teaches you. It's something you bring to it.

Bridging Forward: Identity Before Strategy

This chapter is not about my parents. It's about identity formation. The rule follower and the rule breaker are at opposite ends of the spectrum. They are not abstract personas. They represent the foundation of every investment decision you will ever make. The investor who cannot sit comfortably in disagreement will always be late, buying after the consensus has already priced in the opportunity and selling after the damage is done. The investor who reflexively defies consensus will confuse stubbornness for conviction and miss the moments when the crowd is actually right. Neither instinct, unchecked, builds wealth.

What you are looking for is the honest version of yourself, not the version you present in professional settings or describe on a résumé but the one that shows up when the stakes are real and the outcome is uncertain. That version was formed long before you ever thought about markets. It was formed in the early environments of your life, in the dynamics you observed and absorbed, in what you were rewarded for and what you were penalized for.

My father taught me that structure is not the enemy of freedom. It is what makes freedom sustainable. My mother taught me that authority is not automatically correct and that silence in the face of something wrong is its own kind of failure. I had to learn, over years, how to hold both of those things at once without defaulting entirely to either.

You have your own version of that formation. The question is whether you have examined it. Spend some time with this before you continue reading. Think about where your instincts come from. The more clearly you can see the origins of your own tendencies, the more deliberately you can manage them when the market puts them under pressure. The best investors are not fearless. They are self-aware. That awareness is not something the market teaches you. It is something you bring to the market. And it starts here.

Chapter 4

The Thin Blue Line: Lessons from Law Enforcement and Trauma

Why Stereotypes Exist

Stereotypes don't come from nowhere. They grow from a crumb of truth. Early humans relied on stereotypes for survival. If you assumed the unfamiliar person belonged to a rival tribe, you stayed alive. If you assumed they were harmless and were wrong, the consequences were fatal. Stereotypes began as survival mechanisms. Over time, those mechanisms hardened into shortcuts. Then into narratives. Then, too often, into propaganda and harm.

Growing up as the daughter of a police officer in the 1980s and 1990s, I lived inside stereotypes—both the ones made about me and the ones I absorbed. Most of them still make me smile, because they capture something very real about what it means to grow up a "cop's kid."

The Cop's Kid Reality

Everyone knows the joke: kids of police officers either become cops themselves or end up in jail. It's funny because it's uncomfortably close to the truth. I grew up surrounded by children of police officers, firefighters, and corrections officers. Today, many of them followed their fathers into law enforcement or public service. Others chose paths so diametrically opposed to that world you'd never guess their upbringing. And yes—some did end up behind bars. That kind of polarity isn't random. It's a reaction to the environment.

A Family Shaped by the Badge

My family is full of men in law enforcement, though ironically, the strongest influences weren't my blood relatives. My paternal grandfather was the oldest of six. His two sisters, Sophie and Helen, both married men in law enforcement. My great uncle Joe Karpawich was a corrections officer at the Worcester County Jail. My great uncle Charlie Zimkiewicz was a lieutenant with the Worcester Police Department. Both men influenced my father's decision to become a cop, but it was Charlie who ultimately helped him get the job.

My dad, in turn, became the influence for the next generation. My cousins Anthony and Michael both followed in his footsteps. They credit my father directly for that decision. What stands out isn't just the continuity. It's that the influence came from outside the home, not within it. And that distinction matters.

The Hidden Cost of the Uniform

There are advantages to growing up with a father-in-law enforcement. Seeing your dad in uniform, holding authority, and interacting with influential people, it leaves an impression. But the reality is heavier.

Your father might not come home.

Your father might see things no human should have to see.

And those things don't stay at work.

My dad worked some of the most high-profile cases in the city. His final case before retirement became nationally known as the

"Baby Cut from Womb Murder." But the case that impacted me most happened years earlier.

In the late 1980s, my dad was working a pay job at Maurice the Pants Man when he became the first officer on the scene of a brutal stabbing. The victim had been stabbed multiple times. My dad followed protocol, calling in details and checking for a pulse—only to realize he was covered in the victim's blood.

This was during the height of the AIDS epidemic, when little was understood about transmission. Exposure to blood was terrifying. He had to follow protocol for potential exposure to bloodborne illness. And I remember the fear, the waiting, the stress, that consumed our household. That was my first real understanding that the job didn't belong to him alone. It belonged to all of us.

Normal for Us, Not for Everyone Else

Growing up as a cop's kid meant things that were completely normal to us—and alarming to others.

Occasional joyrides in the cruiser.

Loose bullets in the junk drawer.

Memorizing exactly what to say if I was ever pulled over.

All teenagers get into trouble. But how many have to deal with the cops knowing your dad? And cops love reminding you of that.

Senior year of high school, I helped my best friend dump beer cans into a dumpster behind Newport Creamery. The next day, my dad walked into work and found the entire bag dumped on top of his desk. Getting in trouble is bad. Embarrassing your father in front of his peers is worse.

Trauma as Training

Being part of a law enforcement family creates a baseline level of paranoia—for everyone. Long before the 24-hour news cycle, our family dinners included detailed discussions of what my dad had seen that day. Shootouts. Gang initiations. Armed robberies. Fatal accidents. A decapitation. You grow up understanding the world is dangerous and that risk must be assessed constantly. That awareness never leaves you. It shapes your behavior in ways that you don't expect.

To this day, I carry my purse with me around the house. It's never out of my sight. I scan my surroundings instinctively. I keep distance from buildings to avoid being grabbed. Unseasonable clothing triggers suspicion. A winter parka in June means I'm already looking for the nearest exit. These behaviors seem irrational to others. To me, they are automatic.

Recently, I participated in a self-defense training seminar led by a Sensei from my son's karate dojo. It wasn't the informal instruction my dad had given me growing up. It was real, structured training. It made me realize how deeply ingrained my instincts are.

I catalog faces.

I read body language.

I plan exits without thinking.

Trauma management becomes a daily skill when your parent is a police officer. Coping mechanisms develop early. Awareness becomes reflex. And unexpectedly, those same skills translate to investing.

Your Turn: What Did Fear Teach You About Risk?

Think about the environment you grew up in. Was it stable or unpredictable? Did safety feel guaranteed or like something that had to be constantly maintained? Now think about what happens to you when a market drops when something you believed in starts moving against you and there is no clear signal about when it stops. Do you freeze? Flee immediately? Check prices compulsively? Go emotionally flat? These responses are almost always traceable. The investor who can't hold through volatility often learned early that bad situations escalate without warning and the only safe response is to get out. The investor who takes on excessive risk without adequate caution sometimes grew up in an environment where acknowledging fear felt like weakness. The investor who swings between reckless conviction and sudden paralysis often watched the adults around them do exactly that where money appeared and disappeared unpredictably and financial chaos was simply the baseline. None of these is a character flaw. All of them are survival strategies that made complete sense when they were formed and create predictable problems inside a portfolio. Trauma distorts time horizon, makes the short term feel more real than the long term, and shows up in every financial decision you make whether you are conscious of it or not. I am not asking you to resolve any of this before you continue reading. I am asking you to name it. Awareness is not a cure. It is, however, the only honest place to start.

Calm in Crisis

The skills I developed growing up as the daughter of a cop have become some of my greatest strengths as an investor.

I stay calm in crisis.

I assess risk quickly and unemotionally.

I notice inconsistencies others miss.

I read people—especially under pressure.

Investment decisions are not made in sterile environments. They are made in moments of uncertainty, incomplete information, and emotional noise. The ability to remain grounded while others panic is not theoretical. It is trained.

These experiences aren't just about law enforcement. It's about how trauma shapes perception. Some people underestimate risk because they've never seen real consequences. Others overestimate risk because their nervous system learned early that danger is everywhere. Neither is wrong. But both require awareness.

Your job as an investor is not to eliminate emotion—it's to understand it, manage it, and keep it from hijacking decisions.

Chapter 5

Battered but Unbowed: Overcoming Bullying and Embracing Contrarian Views

Bullying as a Social Force

Bullying is a part of life. It starts early and, if we're honest, it never really ends. Bullying establishes social hierarchy. It identifies difference. It exposes insecurity—sometimes in the victim, often in the aggressor.

In today's world, bullying is harder to escape. Social media delivers it directly to your doorstep. It amplifies small slights and turns them into public judgments. For emotionally sensitive people, even minor acts of bullying can derail an entire day—or worse, an entire sense of self.

Bullying forces conformity. It challenges mental resilience. And if left unchecked, it can shape identity in ways that last a lifetime.

The Origin of the Chip on My Shoulder

I was bullied mercilessly in elementary school. That experience planted a chip on my shoulder that never fully disappeared. Much of my drive—the relentless need to be competent, accomplished, respected—can be traced back to those years. The desire to be chosen. To be worthy. To belong. That need has followed me into adulthood and, at times, made my professional life harder than it needed to be. Wanting to be seen as equal. Wanting respect from peers. Wanting external validation for internal worth. Learning this about myself has been uncomfortable—but necessary.

I remember the moment vividly. Third grade. Lining up for recess. My crush, Matt, was standing next to me with the fourth graders. He smiled and told me he liked my coat—a real rabbit fur hand-me-down from my cousin Julie.

I was floating.

He noticed me.

Sarah noticed too.

Sarah also liked Matt. Emily was her best friend. And Sarah decided, very quickly, that I needed to be put in my place.

It started that afternoon in gym class. My clothes were stolen from my locker, dumped into the shower, and soaked until they were unwearable. I had to go back to class in gym shorts and a T-shirt. My favorite sweater was ruined.

The next day, they brought spray paint to school. While lining up after recess, they sprayed my coat—the same one Matt had complimented. Then the campaign escalated.

"Shana's a dog."

"Ugliest girl in school."

Kids barked at me in the hallways. Posters appeared, mocking my frizzy hair and unibrow. Sarah was cast as the beauty. I was the beast. And the rest of the school followed their lead. I became untouchable, but not in a good way. Untouchable, like the third rail—being friends with me was social suicide.

Isolation and Survival

I ate lunch alone. I sat on a bench near the back entrance of the school during recess, watching other kids play. When I tried out for cheerleading in sixth grade, Emily was the cheer captain. She did everything she could to sabotage me.

When I made the squad—one of only two sixth graders—it enraged her. The pressure intensified. It became relentless. I cried every night. Not because I believed I was ugly. Not because I believed I was unworthy. I cried because it wouldn't stop. Eventually, it became too much. My parents made the decision to move me to a different school so I could have a fresh start. That decision saved me. It let me rewrite my social narrative in a way that I controlled and it set the tone for the person I am now.

The Power of Seeing What's Possible

Leaving wasn't just an escape; it was fuel. I became determined to be everything Sarah and Emily said I couldn't be. I entered the world of modeling and beauty pageants, and it changed my life. I wasn't wildly successful. I didn't win immediately. But pageants introduced me to a world far beyond anything I'd known growing up in Worcester, Massachusetts. The girls I met were larger than life. Smart. Articulate. Ambitious. Community leaders. Exceptional networkers. They weren't just beautiful—they stood for something. That was my real education.

One young woman had a particularly profound impact on me: Maria Menounos. We met as teenagers competing for Miss Massachusetts Teen USA. Because contestant numbers were assigned alphabetically, Maria and I were grouped together for all activities. She was cool. Grounded. Kind. We became real friends—not superficial pageant friends but supportive ones. I remember her telling me she wanted to be an actress. Later, seeing her on Channel One during school felt surreal. She went on to win Miss Massachusetts Teen USA 1996. I was incredibly proud to know her.

Months later, I ran into her at Wachusett Mountain. I was there competing with my ski team. She was there for an appearance. She made a point of telling everyone that I was her friend. And suddenly, my peers saw me differently.

I haven't spoken to Maria in decades. She likely wouldn't recognize me today. But her influence was enormous. She showed me the power of lifting others up. She showed me how to dream beyond geography, background, and expectation. She showed me that big futures belong to real people. That lesson never left me.

Your Turn: Learning to Question What Everyone Else Accepts

Think about the last time you held a real position on something that mattered, that the people around you didn't share. How long before the pressure of being the only one wore you down? Most people capitulate not because they were wrong but because being right in isolation is genuinely uncomfortable. We are wired from childhood to read the social environment and adjust accordingly. In investing, that instinct is one of the most reliable ways to underperform. Now consider what social media has done to it. The same pressure that once operated in a classroom now operates at global scale, in real time, with an algorithm designed to amplify whatever belief is generating the most emotional heat. The crowd that barked at the outlier in the hallway has simply found a bigger platform and the stakes are real. In 2021, retail investors piled into meme stocks not because the fundamentals supported it but because a viral narrative made sitting on the sideline feel like the wrong side of history. Every screenshot of a brokerage account, every person online performing certainty they didn't have, drove decisions that had nothing to do with analysis and everything to do with the need to belong. The next time you feel the pull of a market narrative that is everywhere and carries the social weight of mockery for anyone who questions it, pause and ask three things:

- What would have to be true for this to be wrong?
- Who benefits from this belief being widely held?
- What is the cost to me, specifically of acting as if it is correct when it isn't?

That practice, applied consistently, is what separates the investor who thinks from the investor who scrolls.

Outsiders See What Insiders Miss

This chapter is not just about bullying. It's about outsiders learning to think independently. As an investor, this lesson has been foundational. Investing is not reserved for Ivy League graduates. It is not reserved for men. It is not reserved for people who grew up with wealth. No one has an inherent edge because of where they came from.

The real edge comes from intellectual curiosity, resilience, and the willingness to go against the crowd. Bullied children learn early how dangerous consensus can be. We learn not to trust popularity as proof of truth. We learn to read social dynamics, identify power structures, and survive outside the center. Those skills translate directly into contrarian thinking.

One of my greatest advantages as an investor has been my willingness to approach people I admire without intimidation. Maria taught me that lesson long before I knew what mentorship was. No one is "above" you. They are simply further along. Most successful people are willing to help—if you're willing to ask.

Much of my success has come from learning directly from people who were better, smarter, and more experienced than I was. *Confidence is not arrogance. It's the refusal to self-select out of opportunity. That mindset—earned through hardship—has been a superpower.*

In investing we often talk about crowd psychology, *consensus risk*, and *conviction investing*. But the roots of those concepts often trace back to childhood experiences with belonging or exclusion. If you learned early that standing apart is dangerous, you may cling to consensus. If you learned early that consensus is cruel, you may learn to trust your own judgment. Neither path is wrong—but both must be understood.

True contrarianism is not reflexive opposition. It is informed independence. People who understand that are the ones who achieve great success. People who understand that change the world. Being bullied teaches you something no classroom ever could: popularity is not the same as truth. In investing—and in life—those willing to think independently, seek mentorship, and hold conviction without cruelty are the ones who build something lasting. As you continue reading, we'll begin to move from identity into execution—translating independence into disciplined strategy.

But first, you have to believe you belong at the table.

Because you do.

Chapter 6

Relentless Drive: Competition, Obsession, and the Will to Win

Competition as a Survival Instinct

Competition is human nature.

What began as survival of the fittest evolved into complex cultural rituals—sports, careers, markets, rankings, and status games. You don't have to be an athlete to be competitive, but the most elite performers in any field share a competitiveness that borders on obsession.

I've found myself in rooms with former professional athletes, elite investors, and well-known CEOs. Without fail, they will find a way to make anything a competition.

Anything.

That instinct—to measure, to compare, to win—is a common thread among audacious leaders, top performers, and successful investors. It's not always pretty. But it is powerful.

Competing Without Loving the Game

For most of my youth, I was an elite athlete. Ironically, I didn't actually love the sports I played. What I loved was winning. What drove me wasn't passion for the game; it was an internal demand to be the very best. Whatever I committed to, I had to outwork everyone else. I had to ascend. That meant relentless training, discipline, and effort—regardless of whether joy was involved.

Looking back, this was my first lesson in something I would later recognize in business and investing: *you don't have to love the process to dominate the outcome. But there is a cost to that truth.*

Soccer, Sarah, and the Birth of Obsession

It started with soccer. And it started with Sarah.

Sarah—the same bully who planted the original chip on my shoulder—was also my first true competitor. We played on the same co-ed soccer team when I was seven. The only two girls. We looked similar: long dark hair, cool beige skin, blunt bangs.

She was older. Taller. Better. I hated being her understudy. That one year was the only time we were teammates. From then on, we were opponents. Sarah had the flashy skills, the flip throw-ins, the fancy footwork. I didn't have her finesse. What I had was my mother's fighting spirit and my father's strength. No fear. No hesitation. I played defense. Usually stopper. I was the enforcer. I wasn't the biggest on the field, but I was intense. Intimidating. Sometimes, I crossed the line.

One former opponent still won't speak to me after I broke her leg in a game. I occasionally played with the boys, and they learned quickly not to challenge me—after I dislocated a boy's knee during a spring scrimmage. They called me "The Terminator."

I climbed the competitive ranks quickly, eventually earning an invitation to try out for the U.S. Junior National Team. At tryouts, my confidence bordered on arrogance—until Michelle Akers put me firmly in my place during a scrimmage with the Senior National Team.

I made the team. Then I tore my Achilles. And just like that, it was over.

An Ending I Didn't Mourn

I didn't love soccer. Tearing my Achilles in the summer of 1995 gave me the exit I didn't know how to take myself. I missed playing on the varsity team my senior year of high school. Scholarship offers evaporated—much to my dad's disappointment. I probably exaggerated the length of my recovery to eliminate any hope of returning for elite soccer season. That chapter was closed.

Skiing: Competing Against the Clock—and Myself

Skiing was different. Unlike soccer, I loved it. It wasn't a team sport in the traditional sense. You competed against the clock, the course, and yourself. I loved speed from a very young age.

I raced my first NASTAR course at Loon Mountain when I was six, under the watchful eye of my Uncle Ronnie—a speed demon who raced Masters and immediately saw potential in me. He paid my membership for the Wachusett Mountain Junior Ski Team. We raced in the Junior Olympic league. One of the most famous competitors in the New England junior circuit at the time? Olympic Champion Bode Miller.

Like soccer, I didn't have the build or flexibility for technical events. Slalom wasn't my strength. I was a Super G and Giant Slalom specialist. I never podiumed at the biggest events, but in the high school league and Massachusetts Junior Olympic circuit, I was consistently ranked in the top three. I wanted more—but soccer always disrupted training. There were no scholarships in downhill skiing, so my dad wouldn't allow it to take precedence. Opportunities arose, but I couldn't pursue them.

Skiing was expensive. If I wanted to race, it was on me. So, I worked every winter at Wachusett Mountain to earn my season pass. A local ski shop sponsored me with top equipment. I made it happen.

Crashing—Then Coming Back

My last high school race, I chose to use demo skis—Volkls longer than anything I'd raced on before. I caught a tip at the final gate.

I tumbled through the finish line at freeway speeds, hit the radar gun, broke two ribs, severely bruised my kidneys—and didn't ski again for more than a decade.

Until one day in my mid-20s. Standing in line at Dunkin' Donuts, I overheard an older man complaining that his ski team was short one member. Without thinking, I interrupted. Introduced myself. Explained my background. He accepted immediately.

That season, I remembered how to attack a GS course. I finished first among women in my age group, qualified for the NASTAR National Championships, and won Top Female Skier in the league. I don't do things halfway.

I want to win.

Every time.

All the time.

What changed as I moved from youth into adulthood wasn't my competitiveness—it was the arena. The obsession didn't disappear when sports ended. It simply found new outlets: academics, careers, finance, business-building, leadership. The same internal fire that drove me to dominate on the field became the engine behind my professional life. Deadlines replaced races. Markets replaced scoreboards. Risk replaced physical danger. And the stakes became much higher.

The Fire That Fuels—and Burns

This relentless drive is the source of my greatest strengths and my greatest challenges. Tell me I can't do something, and I will make it my life's work to prove you wrong. It becomes obsession. I won't stop until I have the satisfaction of being right. That fire has powered every success I've had. It has also fueled my anxiety, my impatience, and my intolerance for delay.

It's why I dream big.

It's why I push others to dream bigger.

It's why I get back up after setbacks that should have ended the story.

When people joke that I'm "superhuman," what they're really seeing is not talent—it's refusal.

Your Turn: What Is Actually Driving You?

Before you move forward, sit with this question honestly: is your competitiveness serving you or running you? There is a difference between drive that fuels deliberate, sustainable effort and drive that is really fear in disguise: fear of failure, fear of being overlooked, fear of becoming the person you were told you would be. Both can produce results in the short term. Only one compounds over time. Think about what actually motivates you when things get hard. Is it the genuine love of the work, the intellectual challenge, the craft, the satisfaction of getting something right? Or is it the need to prove something to someone who may not even be watching anymore? Is it excitement about where you are going, or is it the discomfort of standing still? None of these is a wrong answer. But they are important ones, because your motivation determines your staying power. Markets will test your thesis, your patience, your confidence, and your identity, often simultaneously and without warning. The investors who endure are not always the most talented or the most passionate. They are the ones whose reasons for being in the game are strong enough to survive the moments when the game stops being fun. Drive gets you into the arena. Knowing why you are there is what keeps you in it.

Competitive Advantage vs. Self-Destruction

This chapter of my life isn't just about sports. It's about succeeding in life—and investing—at the highest level.

Competitive drive creates advantage. But unchecked, it becomes self-destructive. In investing, the same mindset that pushes you to outperform can also push you into:

- Overtrading
- Overconfidence
- Impatience
- *Risk concentration*

Elite investors don't eliminate competitiveness—they discipline it. They know when to press and when to wait. They understand that sometimes the winning move is restraint. They channel obsession into preparation not reaction. That distinction is everything.

Chapter 7

Accidental Entry: Intuition, Pattern Recognition, and Finding My Way into Finance

When the Numbers Don't Love You Back

Math was never my thing. I failed algebra. Twice.

No one is more amused by my career choice than my algebra teacher, Mr. Gravel.

It wasn't that I disliked math or that I was incapable of understanding it. I simply struggled with subjects rooted entirely in abstraction. When concepts floated without context and symbols detached from anything tangible, I checked out.

Algebra, calculus, and physics were painful.

But statistics, trigonometry, and astronomy? I crushed them. Straight As.

The difference was application. I needed to see how things worked. I needed patterns, systems, movement. When math connected to reality, I excelled.

My academic record reflected that inconsistency. I wasn't obsessed with grades, and I imagine my parents found that frustrating. My performance tracked almost perfectly with my interest level. As I approached college, that lack of focus became a limitation. I didn't know where I wanted to go. I didn't know what I wanted to study.

Finding Direction by Accident

I ended up at UMass Amherst because it was affordable. I changed my major four times before landing on sport management—almost by accident. I loved sports. I loved attention. What could be cooler than talking sports in the media? Once I realized UMass housed one of the top sport management programs in the country, something clicked. Once I found my lane, I thrived.

I wanted to work in sports broadcasting or media relations. I worked at the New England Sports Network (NESN), with the Worcester IceCats of the AHL, and at ESPN's X Games. The sports world became my first real exposure to male-dominated environments filled with ego, hierarchy, and competition.

At NESN, I found a mentor in former NFL Network reporter Kara Henderson. Kara taught me how to navigate rooms full of alpha men—how to hold ground, command respect, and stay composed without shrinking or posturing.

I was convinced I'd end up on the sidelines for ESPN.

The Choice That Changed Everything

But then there was a boy.

Not just any boy. Joe.

I met him when I was 19. The first time I saw him, I was walking back to the dorm with friends. I had never believed in love at first sight—until I walked straight into a wall because I was too distracted by him to see where I was going.

Six-foot-three. Built like a linebacker. Dressed better than any college guy I'd ever seen.

I knew immediately he would matter.

When we finally connected one-on-one, it was magic. For 10 years, he influenced nearly every decision I made—not because he asked me to but because I couldn't imagine a future without him.

My senior year, my media relations professor, Howie Davis, recommended me to Stacey James, head of media relations for the New England Patriots. I was offered a paid internship with the Patriots.

A dream role. A Big Three team. A franchise I grew up idolizing.

I turned it down.

For a boy.

Two weeks before graduation, he left. His dreams didn't include me.

Lost, Then Redirected

I was devastated and unmoored. I scrambled for a job before graduation and landed as an assistant to the president of a corporate travel agency in Boston. I was miserable. I was a terrible executive gopher. My next role was as an account manager at a staffing agency, which was equally uninspiring. I wanted back into sports but didn't know how.

Then one afternoon, my boss walked into my office and asked a simple question: "Can you help me figure out why we can't place anyone at Morgan Stanley Dean Witter?" That question changed everything.

The idea was straightforward. The Morgan Stanley team didn't know me. I was early in my career. I had a business degree (sport management lives under the Isenberg School of Management). I was polished. I could network. I would go in undercover.

Except it didn't go as planned. They offered me the job, which included a significant pay increase. I said yes without hesitation.

Entering Finance Through the Side Door

I never intended to work in finance. I still thought I was headed back to sports. I took the Morgan Stanley role purely because it paid more. I knew *nothing* about markets.

The S&P 500 was a graphic on the nightly news. A stock was an abstract concept. Wall Street was a movie starring Michael Douglas and Charlie Sheen.

I had taken finance and accounting in college but rarely attended class. I showed up for exams, earned Cs, and checked the box required to graduate. If you're reading this and feel intimidated by finance, I was you. The language felt foreign. The systems felt opaque. The people seemed smarter than me. And yet everything changed.

Seeing the System Behind the Noise

Here's the truth: finance *is* complicated. There *is* math involved.

But no, you do not need to be a math genius to succeed.

Once I understood the markets, I realized something profound: *finance is how the world works.*

Everything is touched by markets:

- Interest rates on your car loan, mortgage, and credit cards
- The cost of groceries, clothing, and housing
- Job creation, layoffs, and opportunity

Markets are not numbers—they are systems. And systems are my strength.

Why Finance Finally Clicked

I love puzzles. I love understanding how things function beneath the surface. Finance is the ultimate operating system: alive, dynamic, and human. It's driven by psychology, behavior, incentives, fear, and greed. That's when I became obsessed.

- If you like psychology or sociology, finance is for you.
- If you like engineering or math, finance is for you.
- If you are competitive and enjoy sports, finance is for you.

We saw this during COVID. When sports disappeared, the markets became the game.

Everyone has an edge. The key is understanding *which* edge is yours.

You Belong Here

Let's start by dismantling the myth that finance is reserved for a select few.

You don't need pedigree.

You don't need perfect grades.

You don't need to love math.

You need curiosity. You need pattern recognition.

You need the willingness to engage with complexity instead of running from it. Markets reward those who learn how systems behave under pressure, not those who memorize formulas.

People in my world want you to think they are smarter than you. The truth is they aren't. Fancy designations indicate nothing more than the ability to retain an immense amount of information for a test. It in no way indicates investment acumen.

Your Turn: What Do You Already Know That You Haven't Valued Yet?

You picked up this book for a reason. Maybe finance has always felt like a language spoken just out of earshot, close enough to hear, too technical to follow. Maybe you understand more than you think but have never been given permission to trust it. Either way, you are more prepared for this than you realize. Think about the industry you work in, the products you use every day, the companies you interact with, the problems you see go unsolved in your own field. Think about the trends you have noticed before they became headlines, the businesses you have watched struggle or thrive from the inside, the moments where you thought, before anyone else said it out loud, that something was changing. That is market intelligence. It does not live in a spreadsheet. It lives in your experience. The goal of everything that follows in this book is not to turn you into someone else: an analyst, a portfolio manager, a person with different credentials or a different background. It is to help you see that the curiosity that brought you here, combined with the life you have already lived, is the foundation that everything else gets built on. You don't need to master complexity to understand markets. You need to understand how the world actually works and you have been learning that your entire life. We are about to start connecting those dots.

Finding Your Investing Superpower

Before we move forward, I want to pause, not to test what you know, but to help you notice *what already belongs to you*. The most successful investors are not spreadsheet savants. They are not necessarily the fastest calculators or the most technically trained. What they share is something much simpler and much harder to teach. They understand the businesses they invest in. And they understand them because the work is personal.

Not emotional. Personal.

Why This Matters More than Spreadsheets

Investing is often taught as a purely analytical pursuit. Models, multiples, ratios, forecasts. Those tools matter. We will use them. But they are not the starting point. Markets are made of businesses. Businesses are made of people. And people respond to incentives, fear, opportunity, and pressure.

The investors who endure—the ones who don't panic, don't chase, don't freeze—are the ones who understand *what they're actually investing in*.

They aren't memorizing numbers. They're recognizing behavior.

That understanding rarely comes from textbooks. It comes from lived experience.

Reframing Investing as Personal Knowledge

For me, finance stopped being intimidating the moment I realized it wasn't abstract. It was familiar. Markets weren't mysterious. They were systems. Systems I had been navigating my entire life.

Once I saw that, everything clicked. And that's the reframing I want to carry forward. Investing is not about mastering complexity for its own sake. It's about understanding how the world actually works and why.

Setting the Stage for What Comes Next

Up to this point, this book has focused on *how I was shaped* by work ethic, contrast, trauma, exclusion, competitiveness, and curiosity.

The second half of this book shifts focus.

We move from *who I am* to *what I learned.*

From the psychological foundation to the markets themselves. From identity to events. From instinct to knowledge.

In the chapters ahead, I walk through the market environments, economic moments, and notable world events that deepened my understanding. Not in theory, but in real time. I share how those moments intersected with my life, my career, and my decisions.

Not as history lessons. As lived experience.

Because that's how investing actually works.

A Final Thought Before We Continue

If you take nothing else from this chapter, take this:

- You don't need to become someone else to be a good investor.
- You need to understand *who you already are.*
- Your superpower isn't hiding in a spreadsheet. *It's embedded in your experience.*

From here on, we build on that.

Chapter 8

Discovering Destiny: From Finance Trials to an Unlikely Advisor

The One Who Chose Risk on Purpose

When my career path felt uncertain after graduation, my family encouraged me to choose the safer route.

Just weeks before I was offered a financial advisor role at Morgan Stanley Dean Witter, I told my dad that if I hadn't found an opportunity in sports by the end of the year, I would take the teacher's exam. A pension. A union. Stability. That was what he believed was best for his kids.

I didn't want to be a teacher, but stability sounded appealing. Comforting, even. And then I remembered my Uncle Stan.

Years earlier, I had overheard my dad talking with my Uncle Ronnie about their older brother, Stan. There was an initial public offering (IPO) he had been excited about, and he had urged them to consider investing in it.

Which IPO had gotten him so excited? A little known technology company called Microsoft.

This was the early 1990s, just as the tech boom was beginning. My dad and Uncle Ronnie were commiserating about how they should have listened to him. Uncle Ronnie made a comment that stuck with me: "He can take that risk. He's got plenty of money in the bank."

My Uncle Stan was the black sheep of the family—not in a negative way but in the "one of these things is not like the other" kind of way. He was 15 years older than my dad, raised essentially as an only child. He grew up during the Depression. He lived through a stock market collapse and a world war. That kind of environment shapes a person.

I've never asked him directly, but I'm certain Uncle Stan was driven by scarcity. By a need to understand why the world worked the way it did and how to protect himself from it. While others sought safety, he sought comprehension. That made him different.

Engineering a Different Life

Uncle Stan didn't stumble into success. He designed it. He was a standout football player in high school. He learned the power of networking early. My dad once described it perfectly: "Your Uncle Stan hung out with all the right kids."

His achievements led him to Brown University. He understood something early that would define his life: *it's not just what you know, it's* ***who*** *you know.*

His first job out of college was at a gas station. From there he worked his way up the ranks at Mobil Oil and eventually Amarada-Hess.

By the late 1980s, he had joined the *leveraged buyout (LBO)* wave and with two partners bought Meenan Oil Company—at the time, the largest home heating oil company in the United States. In 1986, the *Worcester Evening Gazette* ran a feature on him titled: "From the Football Field to the Boardroom: Ex-City Grid Star Buys Oil Firm."

When my grandmother died in 1995, I found the article among her belongings. I laminated it and have carried it in my wallet ever since (see Figure 8.1).

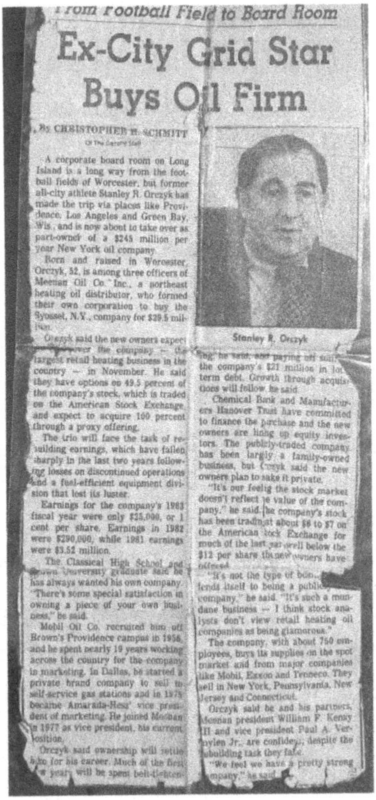

[illegible]rom Football Field to Board Room

Ex-City Grid Star Buys Oil Firm

By CHRISTOPHER R. SCHMITT
Of The Gazette Staff

A corporate board room on Long Island is a long way from the football fields of Worcester, but former all-city athlete Stanley R. Orczyk has made the trip via places like Providence, Los Angeles and Green Bay, Wis., and is now about to take over as part-owner of a $245 million per year New York oil company.

Born and raised in Worcester, Orczyk, 52, is among three officers of Meenan Oil Co. Inc., a northeast heating oil distributor, who formed their own corporation to buy the Syosset, N.Y., company for $29.5 million.

Orczyk said the new owners expect [illegible] the company — the largest retail heating business in the country — in November. He said they have options on 49.5 percent of the company's stock, which is traded on the American Stock Exchange, and expect to acquire 100 percent through a proxy offering.

The trio will face the task of rebuilding earnings, which have fallen sharply in the last two years following losses on discontinued operations and a fuel-efficient equipment division that lost its luster.

Earnings for the company's 1983 fiscal year were only $25,000, or 1 cent per share. Earnings in 1982 were $290,000, while 1981 earnings were $3.52 million.

The Classical High School and Brown University graduate said he has always wanted his own company. "There's some special satisfaction in owning a piece of your own business," he said.

Mobil Oil Co. recruited him off Brown's Providence campus in 1956, and he spent nearly 19 years working across the country for the company in marketing. In Dallas, he started a private brand company to sell to self-service gas stations and in 1975 became Amarada-Hess' vice president of marketing. He joined Meenan in 1977 as vice president, his current position.

Orczyk said ownership will settle [illegible] for his career. Much of the first [illegible] years will be spent belt-tighten[illegible]

Stanley R. Orczyk

[illegible] he said, and paying off [illegible] the company's $21 million in lo[illegible] term debt. Growth through acquisi[illegible]tions will follow, he said.

Chemical Bank and Manufacturers Hanover Trust have committed to finance the purchase and the new owners are lining up equity investors. The publicly-traded company has been largely a family-owned business, but [illegible] said the new owners plan to take it private.

"It's our feeling the stock market doesn't reflect [illegible] value of the company," he said. [illegible] company's stock has been trading at about $6 to $7 on the American [illegible] Exchange for much of the last [illegible] well below the $12 per share the new owners have offered.

"It's not the type of bus[illegible] lends itself to being a public[illegible] company," he said. "It's such a mundane business — I think stock analysts don't view retail heating oil companies as being glamorous."

The company, with about 750 employees, buys its supplies on the spot market and from major companies like Mobil, Exxon and Tenneco. They sell in New York, Pennsylvania, New Jersey and Connecticut.

Orczyk said he and his partners, Meenan president William F. Kenny III and vice president Paul A. Vernylen Jr., are confident, despite the rebuilding task they face.

"We feel we have a pretty strong company," he said.

Figure 8.1 Newspaper clipping from the *Worcester Evening Gazette* of my Uncle Stan's unusual career trajectory

Seeing the Life I Wanted

Uncle Stan was more of a presence than a participant in my childhood. His ambition took him everywhere—Green Bay, Pasadena, Dallas—before he finally settled on Long Island. He went where opportunity was. He was never afraid to leave home. No one else in my family lived that way.

When "Junior" came to visit, my grandmother insisted everything be perfect. Her hair had to be done. Makeup flawless. A new dress for the occasion. Family dinners were carefully planned and held at sophisticated establishments like Maxwell Silverman's or the Beechwood Inn. Everything shifted when he was around. Even as a kid, I knew that was the life I wanted.

Making the Call That Changed Everything

When I was offered the job at Morgan Stanley, my dad was deeply uneasy. Commission-based compensation felt risky. Unstable. I wanted advice from someone who actually understood that world. So, at 22 years old, I picked up the phone and called my Uncle Stan. It was the first real conversation we'd ever had.

Unbeknownst to me, my cousin Karen already worked at Morgan Stanley, an interest rate strategist and executive director on the *swaps desk*. Uncle Stan knew exactly what I was stepping into. He didn't hesitate. He told me finance offered unlimited opportunity. He told me to take the job. With his blessing, my dad finally relented. I accepted the position.

Finance Is Still High School

The very next call I made was to an old high school friend, Brian. He worked on Wall Street. Not figuratively. Literally. I was excited to tell him I'd be joining Morgan Stanley Dean Witter. His response was immediate and dismissive: "Might as well be an associate at The Gap. Financial advisors don't matter in my world—it's a joke of a role."

That comment never left me. It was the moment I realized finance was just high school all over again—only with better suits and bigger egos. My entire career has been a sustained rebuttal to that statement.

Learning the Language from the Inside

When I started at Morgan Stanley, the routine was rigid. All advisor trainees were required to arrive early for the morning call, an internal video feed of the analyst meeting, which started *promptly* at 7:30 a.m. Eastern Time.

This was the height of the *tech bubble*. Morgan Stanley's sell-side strategists were rock stars: Byron Wien, Barton Biggs, Phil Roth. Mary Meeker was practically a Wall Street deity. (Mary Meeker was one of Wall Street's most influential technology analysts during the 1990s tech boom, earning the nickname "Queen of the Net" for her bullish and widely followed research on Internet companies.)

There were 20 financial advisors in the Worcester office. Only one was a woman.

I was number two. In a world ruled by men, Mary Meeker became my North Star. I read every research note she published. Took meticulous notes during her presentations. A woman besting her male counterparts. Demanding their respect. That was what I wanted to do someday.

I often describe that time as learning Spanish by living in Spain. Those morning meetings were critical to achieving fluency. The more I sat through them, the more I began to understand the language of the markets.

Passing the Gatekeepers

New advisors spent their first 60 days studying for the securities licensing exams: *FINRA Series 7, 66*, and *31*. You needed a 70% to pass, and you got only one chance. There was an unspoken rule: pass comfortably but not too well. Scores above 80 were frowned upon. That meant you were "too academic."

I passed with a 78.

Finding My Edge by Specializing

I didn't love being a financial advisor.

Business development meant cold calling from the phone book. It was a numbers game—300 dials for four appointments, one client. If you've seen the movie *Boiler Room*, you understand the culture. We weren't trying to pitch a pump-and-dump scheme, but the approach was the same. "Dialing for dollars" was the key to success.

I was young. I was a woman. I was underestimated.

They called me "Barbie" behind my back. One senior advisor propositioned me at the Christmas party. When I declined, he told me I was a distraction, that my attire was inappropriate, and that I would fail unless I slept my way to the top. I was mortified.

I was also furious.

So, I stopped trying to fit in and started trying to out-specialize. *529 College Savings plans* were new. Complex. Ignored. I made them my domain.

I built my entire book of business around them, became the top-producing new advisor in my office, and ranked in the top 20 nationwide in my training class. I've repeated this strategy of finding what others overlook and mastering it ever since.

Discovering I Could Actually Invest

Despite my success as an advisor, what I loved most was research. I built detailed stock monitors on Bloomberg. I followed companies obsessively for clients and for myself.

Friends of mine were obsessed with video games and could not stop talking about the incredible new 3D graphics made possible through something called GPUs. I paid attention. I began researching who were the key players behind this new technology.

That's how I found NVIDIA in 2001.

No model. No charts. Just observation.

I didn't invest personally. I couldn't afford the risk. I was still shaped by my father's risk-averse worldview. So, I recommended it to clients and tracked it in my paper portfolio instead. Turns out, I was pretty good at this investing thing.

Turning Experience into Investing Edge

I found my passion in the financial markets. My intellectual curiosity was fully engaged by the mysteries of the markets. It turned out I also had a knack for building top-performing portfolios for my clients. This chapter isn't trying to convince you to follow the same career path I did. It's to help you recognize where your advantage might already be hiding.

Most people assume successful investors start with capital, credentials, or technical brilliance. In reality, they start with understanding—and that understanding almost always comes from lived experience. Everyone has the ability to do the same. You just need to know how. The sections that follow cover seven main tenets for finding your investing edge.

What My Story Means for Yours

I did not share the story of this chapter to be inspiring. I shared it because every element of it, the uncle who took risks nobody else in the family would, the dismissive comment from a friend on Wall Street, the 529 plans nobody wanted to sell, the NVIDIA call that came from listening rather than modeling, contains a principle that applies directly to you. The sections that follow are not abstract investing theory. They are the specific, repeatable lessons I extracted from my own experience, reframed so you can apply them to yours. Read them as instructions, not observations.

Stop Looking for the "Right" Background

You do not need a finance degree, a Wall Street pedigree, or perfect grades to be a good investor. What you need is context.

Ask yourself:

- What industries do I understand because I've worked in them, depended on them, or lived alongside them?
- What products, services, or systems do I interact with regularly?
- Where do I notice change before it shows up in headlines?

My edge didn't come from spreadsheets. It came from noticing how people actually used technology, where money flowed, and which parts of the system were ignored. Your edge will come from where you've been paying attention your whole life.

Risk Is Personal—So Learn to Name Yours

Risk tolerance isn't theoretical. It's emotional, historical, and deeply personal. My father avoided risk because stability was survival. My uncle embraced risk because understanding the system made it manageable. Neither approach was wrong but only one aligned with the life I wanted.

Ask yourself:

- What risks feel terrifying—and why?
- What risks feel intuitive or manageable?
- Where am I avoiding opportunity out of inherited fear rather than actual danger?

Good investors don't eliminate fear. They understand where it comes from and adjust accordingly.

Specialization Beats Generalization Every Time

When I was underestimated, I didn't try to compete everywhere. I found a corner others ignored and owned it. That strategy applies directly to investing. You don't need to understand everything. You need to understand something deeply.

For example:

- If you work in healthcare, you likely understand inefficiencies others miss.
- If you're in education, you see where funding flows and where it doesn't.
- If you're in technology, logistics, retail, or real estate, you already see patterns forming.

Pick one area. Go deep. Let familiarity become insight.

Pay Attention to the World, Not Just the Markets

I found NVIDIA not by running models but by listening to people around me and noticing what captured attention before Wall Street cared. Markets move after behavior changes—not before.

Make it a habit to ask:

- What are people excited about?
- What are they frustrated by?
- What are they adopting without thinking twice?

Investing starts long before a ticker symbol ever appears on your screen.

Don't Confuse Gatekeepers with Authorities

The dismissive comment from my friend on Wall Street was a gift, even if it didn't feel like one at the time. It revealed something important: every industry has gatekeepers who confuse status with insight.

You don't need permission to learn. You don't need validation to observe. You don't need approval to think independently. Some of the best investors I know entered through side doors, back doors, or accidental openings—just like I did.

Curiosity Is a Skill—Train It

What changed my life wasn't a sudden burst of intelligence. It was sustained curiosity. I read. I watched. I tracked things without owning them. I treated the market like a living system to be understood, not a puzzle to be solved quickly.

You can do the same:

- Follow companies without investing in them.
- Track trends without acting on them.
- Observe cycles without trying to time them.

Understanding compounds long before money does.

The Goal Is Not Confidence—It's Competence

Confidence without competence is dangerous. Competence creates confidence naturally. You don't need to feel "ready" to start learning markets. Read anyway. Watch anyway. Ask anyway.

Over time, something shifts. What once felt foreign starts to feel familiar. What once felt intimidating starts to feel navigable. What once felt exclusive starts to feel accessible.

That's how real investors are built.

Your Turn: Bringing It All Together

As you read on, I encourage you to keep asking one question: where does my life intersect with the markets—and what do I already know that I haven't valued yet? That's where your edge lives.

This chapter is an invitation to reframe how you think about investing. Not as a technical exercise. Not as an elite club. Not as a personality type you either have or don't. But as a process of recognition.

Chapter 9

Standing Strong: Resilience Through 9/11 and Personal Crisis

A Commitment to Authenticity

I'm in my late 40s, and my life has not been easy.

Sometimes I wonder if people keep their distance from me—not because they don't care but because they see the accumulation of struggle and think, I don't want that kind of chaos touching my life. My friend Brittany calls me a superhero. She means it as a compliment.

It's a title I'd gladly give back.

When you survive enough hardship, people expect you to be endlessly strong. Unbreakable. Stoic. They assume resilience means you don't feel the weight of things. The truth is, broken is where I live most of the time. I just refuse to let it stop me from continuing to move forward.

I don't believe in performative strength. I believe in honesty, even when it makes people uncomfortable. Especially then.

The Pattern I Couldn't Ignore

My adult life has followed a pattern I didn't recognize at first. The more excited I become about the future—the more aligned I feel with where I'm heading—the more life seems to humble me. Over time, I learned to use those moments as mirrors for growth.

But sometimes the lesson comes after real pain. For me, that pattern began in 2001.

When the Past Reappeared

In the early days at Morgan Stanley Dean Witter, I was completely absorbed in my studies. Learning the language of markets, trying to prove I belonged. Then I came face to face with my past.

Joe.

He had enlisted in the Army and was back in Massachusetts after boot camp, working as a scientist at the U.S. Army Research Institute of Environmental Medicine (USARIM). It felt like fate. I had finally found a career path that energized me, and the love of my life had returned.

He brought magic back into my world. I was on a high that seemed impossible to come down from.

One Perfect Week

After passing my licensing exams, I had one week off before heading to New York City for Morgan Stanley's New Hire Training Program. I would live and work in the city for the entire month of September alongside peers from across the country.

Before that, I flew to San Antonio to see Joe, who was completing specialized training at Fort Sam Houston. I still remember arriving at the gate and seeing him waiting for me, a dozen roses in hand.

That week was perfect. We talked about the future. We visited a local jeweler for engagement ring inspiration. We imagined a life that finally made sense. When I left for New York on September 9, 2001, I was floating. I had no idea how much would change in less than 48 hours.

Reporting for Duty at the World Trade Center

I was thrilled to be in New York City. It was my first real experience of Manhattan, and I was intoxicated by it. I had watched enough *Sex and the City* to feel like I'd stepped into something glamorous and important.

While others were content building lives in Worcester, Massachusetts, I was eager to be near power. Near the heartbeat of Wall Street. Morgan Stanley's offices were in the World Trade Center, 2 World Trade Center to be exact.

The reception area sat on the 61st floor. Mahogany everywhere. An employee cafeteria that felt like money lived there. My training classroom was on the 65th floor. There were more than 300 trainees, divided into groups of 50. Day 1 was orientation. Day 2 would begin with presentations from the firm's biggest names.

September 11, 2001, was a flawless Tuesday morning. Warm. Clear. Perfect.

The Last Normal Moment

I woke up early, eager for the day. The first session featured Morgan Stanley's chief market technician, Phil Roth. I knew nothing about technical analysis, and I was excited to learn. Our group wasn't in the main room—we had a live feed. I came prepared with research notes covered in handwritten questions.

No one else raised their hand. I was the only trainee willing to ask questions over a glorified intercom system. Looking back, they weren't brilliant questions—but I wanted to understand. Phil was grateful for the engagement. The session ended early. That extra break would change everything.

When the World Fractured

I went to the kitchenette to grab hot tea—the room temperature was set low to keep us alert. On my way back to my desk, I stopped to talk with a classmate standing by the window, admiring the view of the Statue of Liberty.

Ash began to fall.

We were confused. What is that? Then a giant ball of fire streamed past the window. The room erupted. "GET THE FUCK OUT."

I ran to my desk and grabbed my research reports, notebook, and purse—an instinct that makes no sense now but felt necessary then. Morgan Stanley's security team, led by Rick Rescorla, instructed us to ignore the intercom orders that said to return to our desks. Their message was clear: continue the evacuation.

The stairwell was packed. We moved slowly. I was somewhere around the 30th floor when the second plane hit our building. The rest of the day is a blur. It exists only in fragments of my memories.

When Markets Learned Fear

This chapter is not meant to recount the horrors of that day in detail. That story is well documented. What matters is this: surviving 9/11 was trauma. PTSD is real. Being physically present for one of the worst terrorist attacks in U.S. history changes you. It changed me. And it changed the world.

The events of that day set my life on a path I could not have predicted. They also reshaped financial markets, investor psychology, and global policy for decades.

The tech bubble had already begun to crack. 9/11 shattered what remained of the illusion that markets were invincible. The glamorous excess of the 80s and 90s was over. The world had changed. Adapt or perish. Decades of professional experience suddenly meant less than the ability to think differently. Bonds mattered again. Risk mattered again. The 60/40 portfolio became gospel. New titans emerged. Bill Gross. Hedge fund managers replaced the glamorous mutual fund managers of the past: Steve Cohen, David Tepper, Jim Simons, Ken Griffin, Bill Ackman, David Einhorn, Cliff Asness. Markets had entered a new era. And somehow, improbably, that shift created space for someone like me.

Your Turn: What Did Your Hardest Moment Build in You?

Think about the worst thing that has happened to you. Not a disappointment or a setback, the *real* one. The event or the season that broke something open, that divided your life into before and after, that you would never have chosen and cannot fully explain to anyone who wasn't inside it. Now ask yourself honestly: what exists in you today, because of that experience, that did not exist before? Not what you lost you already know that inventory by heart. What did you gain? What did you learn to see that you could not see when life felt predictable and safe? What capacity did you develop because you had no choice but to develop it? Resilience is not a personality trait you are born with. It is built, almost always involuntarily, in the moments that demand more from you than you believed you had. The investors who navigate uncertainty most effectively are not the ones who have been spared difficulty. They are the ones who have already survived it and know, because they have proof, that they can function through things that feel devastating. Whatever your version of that experience is, it did not just happen to you. In ways you may not have fully accounted for yet, it prepared you. The question worth sitting with is not why it happened. It is what you are going to do with what it made you.

Resilience as an Investing Skill

Tragedy is a part of life. You can let it break you or you can let it teach you a lesson. It builds a resilient mindset, and as it turns out resilience is an important market skill. Real investing is forged during periods of uncertainty, fear, and structural change—not during long bull markets when everything works.

Here's what 9/11 taught me that applies directly to you:

- Markets can change overnight.
- What worked before may stop working entirely.
- Experience matters less than adaptability.
- Psychological resilience becomes a competitive advantage.
- Investors who survive and thrive are not the ones who avoid pain. They are the ones who learn how to function through it.

Trauma recalibrates perspective. After you've lived through something that breaks the illusion of permanence, you stop assuming tomorrow will look like today. You question consensus. You prepare for dislocation. That mindset, while painful, is powerful. It forces humility. It sharpens awareness. It builds durability. And durability is what investing actually requires.

Every experience described in this book has been building toward a way of seeing the world that applies far beyond my own life. Identity, background, hardship, curiosity, and resilience all shape how we interpret risk, opportunity, and change. Markets are no different. Once you understand that investing is not abstract—but human, behavioral, and deeply contextual—you stop trying to predict outcomes and start learning how systems actually respond under pressure.

Markets are never static. They move, fracture, adapt, and reassemble in response to real events and real people making real decisions. When you learn to observe those movements with clarity instead of fear, you develop a skill that compounds over time. This is the ground everything else rests on.

Resilience is not about being unbreakable. It's about continuing—intentionally and with awareness—after something has changed you. That capacity to adapt, reassess, and stay engaged is what allows people to build lasting success in uncertain environments. Markets reward those who can do exactly that. And this foundation is something anyone can build on.

Chapter 10

Conviction Under Fire: Authority, Doubt, and the Making of an Investor

Earning a Seat at the Table

Becoming a financial advisor ignited my passion for financial markets but not because of the job itself. The role was sales and relationship management. It paid the bills, built confidence, and taught me how to communicate. But the work that energized me lived elsewhere. I was fascinated by markets, businesses, and how capital actually moved. I had found my direction. Now I had to build a path toward it.

The problem was my résumé. I wasn't going to be handed responsibility for billion-dollar portfolios with two years of sales experience and a bachelor's degree in an unrelated field. If I wanted to do the work I cared about, I needed to rebuild my profile deliberately.

That realization became my first adult lesson in investing: wanting something isn't enough, you have to become credible for it.

Slipping Through the Side Door

I decided the most logical next step was an MBA from a top-rated business school. There was only one problem: I didn't have the credentials to get into one. So, I did what I've always done.

I looked for a way in through the side door. I applied to several top business schools in the Boston area. Only one had a loophole I could use.

Bentley University's McCallum School of Business offered multiple degree programs, including a highly competitive MBA. That year, however, their Global Financial Analysis program had very few applicants. I leaned into one of my strongest assets: communication.

Years of pageantry had made me an exceptional interviewer. I knew how to tell a story, articulate intent, and connect quickly. In my admissions interview, I impressed the director enough that he wanted to find a way to admit me. I amended my application and was accepted into the Global Financial Analysis program with a clear path to transfer into the MBA program later, which is exactly what I did.

Moving Closer to the Work That Mattered

With business school underway, my next objective was clear: transition from sales into research. The most logical route was a firm that offered both and allowed interaction across functions. Fidelity Investments was right in my backyard, and opportunities on their sales desk were plentiful. I took one. But this time, I had a plan.

I knew I was good at building portfolios. I just needed the right people to see it. So, I made myself memorable. I sat in the front row of every presentation by a strategist or portfolio manager. I stayed late to ask questions. I focused on learning, building rapport, and being consistently visible. Within a year, I was invited to an informational interview for an entry-level research role.

I impressed the department head enough that they created a job for me. I had to take a pay cut. But five years into a career, that's survivable. Ten years in, it's much harder. I wasn't married. Joe and I had fallen apart after 9/11 when long distance and shifting priorities took their toll. I had no children. My responsibilities were my cat and my bills. I knew where I wanted to go, and this pivot was part of the plan.

When Talent Isn't Enough

Here's the part no one talks about. Being good at picking investments does not automatically make you good at research.

My entire life, I had relied on communication, intuition, and momentum. Research demanded something different: patience, precision, and obsessive attention to detail. I struggled. I rushed. I missed things. I moved faster than the work required. I was curious but not yet disciplined. At my first annual review, the message was clear: develop this skill quickly, or your research career would end before it started.

That was humbling. And necessary.

The Apple Pitch That Changed Everything

I worked relentlessly to improve and used every opportunity to learn from Fidelity's portfolio managers. In the winter of 2007, I was invited to interview for an equity research analyst role at Fidelity Management & Research (FMR), the most exclusive group at the firm. I made it to the final round.

Each candidate was required to present one or two stock ideas to current portfolio managers. Eager to impress, I chose the stock I had the highest conviction in: Apple Inc. (AAPL). At the time, Apple was trading between $2 and $3. I had built a detailed analysis outlining how Apple was creating an ecosystem; hardware, software, content, and brand loyalty unlike anything else in the market. iPods dominated music. iTunes had become the gatekeeper as the music industry cracked down on file sharing. The MacBook was gaining share. And there was buzz about a new device: the iPhone.

My thesis was simple: Apple had built a cult following among younger consumers, and everything worked better when connected. My model produced a 36-month price target of $50.

I was confident in my work and walked into my interview ready to crush it.

When Conviction Meets Authority

The first portfolio manager focused less on my analysis and more on idea generation. I felt encouraged. The second interview was with one of the most respected portfolio managers at the firm, the leader of a massive and highly successful mid cap growth fund. I delivered my pitch with authority; I knew this was going to be a home run.

When I finished, he looked at me and said it was the worst pitch he'd ever heard. He told me I was delusional to believe Apple could go from $2.50 to $50 based on a product that could never compete with BlackBerry.

I didn't get the job.

The Advice That Mattered

A month later, I asked my mentor, Tom Allen, what I could have done differently. After a pause, he said, "You should have pitched a more conservative stock—one with a more reasonable price target." I felt crushed. Then he added something else. "Don't give up. Fidelity isn't the only place to work. Boston isn't the only place to live. You should widen your search—and consider relocating." I loved working at Fidelity. I loved living in Boston. Begrudgingly, I followed his advice.

That week, I sent my résumé to every firm in the country with an active research analyst opening. I had Chicago in mind. The universe had other plans—plans that required a stop in Seattle and a plot twist I didn't see coming.

The Real Lesson Apple Taught Me

That interview was the first time someone I deeply respected made me feel small. He made me question my instincts and wonder if I didn't belong. And for a while, it worked. I hesitated. I second-guessed. I learned how easy it is to abandon conviction when authority disagrees with you. It didn't take long before Apple taught me otherwise.

Having a title, pedigree, or a multibillion-dollar fund does not guarantee superior insight. Vision matters. Instinct matters. And so does timing. The day I pitched Apple, it closed at $2.54. A $500 investment that day would be worth more than $45,000 today.

Your Turn: When Someone You Respected Said You Were Wrong

Think about a time someone you admired—a mentor, a manager, an expert whose opinion genuinely mattered to you—dismissed an idea you believed in. Not a casual disagreement, but the kind of rejection that landed hard enough to make you question your own judgment. How did it feel in the moment? Did you defend your position or go quiet? Did you walk away still believing you were right, or did their authority override your instincts before you had a chance to think it through? And here is the harder question: looking back now, were they actually right or did you let the weight of who they were substitute for the quality of their argument? There is a version of humility that is genuinely healthy: the kind that keeps you learning, that forces you to stress-test your thinking, that prevents conviction from hardening into arrogance. And there is a version that is actually just deference, the instinct to hand your confidence over to whoever

(continued)

(continued)

has the biggest title in the room. The difference matters enormously in investing and in every other domain where independent judgment is required. The goal is not to become someone who never listens. It is to become someone who can separate a good challenge from an intimidating one and hold their ground when the evidence still supports it, regardless of who is doing the challenging.

Turning Setbacks into Skill

The most important lesson here is the importance of earning credibility without losing conviction. Here's how it applies to you:

- Build the profile you need, not the one you're handed. Credentials matter but initiative matters more.
- Play to your strengths, then shore up your weaknesses. Awareness accelerates growth.
- Expect to be wrong about process before you're wrong about ideas. Skill development is non-negotiable.
- Don't confuse authority with infallibility. Titles don't equal truth.
- Learn when to refine your presentation without abandoning your insight.

Great investors learn how to balance humility with conviction. That balance takes time and mistakes. It was this experience that marked my shift from entry to refinement. From ambition to capability. From instinct to discipline. From wanting to belong to earning my place.

This is the work beneath the work, and it's what makes everything that follows possible.

It's important to remember this: *being wrong is part of becoming good.*

But losing trust in your own thinking is far more dangerous than missing a trade. The real edge comes from learning how to improve your process without abandoning your vision. That's a skill worth earning.

Chapter 11

Crossing Borders: A West Coast Move and a New Perspective on Investing

Leverage and Illusion: When the System Breaks Before You Do

Like so many others at the time, I found myself captivated by the housing market. Record-low interest rates, easy credit, and rapidly falling barriers to mortgage approval had turned residential real estate into the hottest game in town. It felt inevitable. Everyone was doing it. Everyone was winning.

My dad had always preached the value of homeownership. In his mind, financial success wasn't fully realized until you owned a home. I had a bit of savings and a growing career, and I didn't want to miss what felt like a once-in-a-lifetime opportunity. So I leaned in.

When Approval Feels Like Validation

I became obsessed with real estate websites, imagining granite countertops and spacious master bedrooms. Applying for a mortgage was almost laughably easy. I had seen Countrywide Mortgage commercials everywhere, so I filled out their online application. Much to my surprise, I was quickly approved for a $250,000 mortgage. Pre-approval letter in hand, I called my friend Jeff, and the house hunt began.

I focused on townhomes, low maintenance, but more grown-up than apartment living. It didn't take long to find the perfect place in Uxbridge, Massachusetts. Only 15 minutes away from my office in Smithfield, Rhode Island. Easy access to Boston by commuter rail. It felt responsible. Strategic. Smart.

Sitting down with my mortgage broker, I ran the numbers carefully. I wanted my payment to be less than $1,000 a month. The townhome came in at $1,200—higher than my comfort level but still manageable. We made a strong offer. It was accepted with minimal negotiation. I was euphoric.

When the Paperwork Lies

On closing day, I arrived with a cashier's check in hand. My attorney, Tom, a close friend, was giving me the friends and family discount. I was mindful of his time and didn't press him for extra hand-holding. The closing went smoothly. Keys in hand, I drove straight to my new home, smiling the entire way. Then my phone rang.

It was Tom.

"I'm so sorry to tell you this," he said, "but we need to redo the closing." The bank had shorted the wire by more than $20,000. Assuming it was an error, Tom covered the shortfall himself to avoid jeopardizing the deal. It turned out to be the wrong decision.

The next morning, Tom called Countrywide to investigate. The explanation was simple and devastating. The original underwriter had calculated everything, assuming a 20% down payment. I had only put down 10%. I had two choices:

- Come up with an additional $20,000
- Accept a new amortization schedule

Because Tom had already wired the funds to the seller, we couldn't unwind the deal. I didn't have $20,000. I was trapped.

The revised mortgage carried a $2,200 monthly payment well beyond the income limits for Fannie or Freddie compliance. The bank was stuck holding the loan. I was stuck holding the bill.

Things deteriorated quickly.

After the second closing, Tom said something that still echoes in my mind: "I don't think you're the first—or the last—borrower they've done this to. If this goes south, you probably have a lawsuit."

Personal Leverage Meets Market Reality

I was drowning in mortgage debt, but something else was happening at the same time. The résumés I'd sent out were working. I began landing interviews for equity research roles. Capital Group in Los Angeles, William Blair in Chicago. Then something unexpected landed in my inbox: an Equity Portfolio Analyst role at a *hedge fund* in Seattle. The firm was Russell Investments. At the time, all I knew about Russell was the Russell 2000 Index.

Entering the "Dark Side"

I knew nothing about hedge funds. I worked at one of the largest long-only asset managers in the world, often positioned against short sellers. Hedge funds, in my mind, were arrogant, predatory, and detached from the real economy. They were the dark side of investing. So why was Russell interested in me?

Russell was struggling to fill the role because of one non-negotiable requirement: proficiency in MPI Stylus, a complex and obscure analytics platform. I had listed it on my résumé. It didn't matter that I had no hedge fund experience. It didn't matter that I wasn't a quant. MPI Stylus took years to learn—and they didn't have years to wait. Suddenly, I was the strongest candidate for the job.

When Life Accelerates Without Warning

The process moved fast. Within a week of their initial email, I was boarding a plane in Providence, flying first class to Seattle. I had never flown west of the Mississippi. Never flown first class. And just like that, my world expanded.

Black car service. A five-star hotel. A whirlwind day of interviews. At one point, the managing director mentioned he'd Googled me and found my pageant history. He asked whether I worried about employers finding bikini photos online. I reframed it immediately. Pageants had taught me composure, communication, and resilience.

That night, as we admired Mount Rainier from the Columbia Tower Club, Mary, the hiring manager, offered me the job and a substantial pay raise.

I didn't accept right away. Seattle was far. Hedge funds weren't the dream. I wanted to be an equity research analyst. I wanted to be the next Peter Lynch. This wasn't the plan.

Mary encouraged me to take the weekend. Russell had scheduled my departure for Sunday on purpose. It was Memorial Day weekend, and they wanted me to experience the city. When I returned home Sunday night, reality made the decision for me. I walked into the townhome I couldn't afford and discovered the stove no longer worked and the fridge needed a new compressor.

I called Mary the following Tuesday and accepted the job.

The Past Makes One Last Appearance

Before leaving, I sent a blast email to my contacts announcing the move. I didn't realize Joe was still on the list. The weekend before my departure, my family threw a going-away party. As it wound down, my phone rang. The voice on the other end was unmistakable. I'd know that thick New York accent anywhere. It was Joe.

He congratulated me and asked to take me to dinner that night. It had been almost two years since I had last seen him. Without hesitation I said yes, hung up the phone, turned to my mom and said, "I have to go." She was not pleased when I told her why. "Shana, that man's hold on you isn't healthy; you can't just drop everything because he wants to see you." I knew she was right, but I didn't care.

I went.

Two hours later, we sat across from each other at Pub 99, talking until closing time. I missed him. I couldn't help myself. "Are you seeing anyone?" I asked. He was quick to respond no. Suddenly I wished I wasn't moving 3,000 miles away.

I invited him to the *real* bon voyage party. The one my sorority sisters were throwing for me. He asked me to email him the details. I did as soon as I got home. The next morning, I woke to an email that shattered me. From his wife. His pregnant wife.

And just like that, I was suddenly very ready to leave.

A Clean Break and a New World

My mom, my dog, and I drove across the country. Five days, start to finish. Something everyone should do at least once. Two days after arriving in Seattle, I started at Russell. I was completely out of my comfort zone.

My first assignment: build a regression model to decompose returns for an asset-based lending fund that had gated redemptions. I didn't even understand the question. It didn't matter anyway; I just nodded my head and got to work.

The analysis I was running would later become common for hedge fund replication. At the time, we weren't replicating; we were trying to understand exposures so we could hedge risk while waiting for our redemption request to be fulfilled.

When I asked why we couldn't sell the position, the answer was simple: "No liquidity." That was my first real glimpse behind the curtain. Within a month, my view of hedge funds changed completely. They weren't the villains. They were the canary in the coal mine.

The first domino.

Recognizing Fragility Early

Hidden leverage and invisible risk. That's the lesson. Here's how it applies to you:

- Easy approval is not the same as safety.
- Liquidity matters more than price.
- Leverage magnifies small mistakes into life-altering ones.
- Systems often break quietly before they fail loudly.
- Skills you don't value may be the ones that save you.
- Understanding risk means understanding where fragility hides.

As I look back on that time of my life, the reality becomes crystal clear. The mortgage mistake wasn't just personal—it was systemic.

And stepping into hedge funds wasn't a moral compromise; it was an education. It was an education that was almost perfectly timed with what remains the most significant economic event of my lifetime.

This was the moment I stopped seeing markets as abstract and started seeing where they crack first. That awareness would change everything. The Queen of Alternatives began to take shape in August 2007. And there was no turning back.

Chapter 12

Market Meltdown: Navigating the GFC and Embracing Transformation

Crises Never Arrive Slowly

In all my years in the financial industry, I've learned that crises never happen slowly, and they are rarely forecasted in advance. Sure, there are media contributors who take the market's temperature. *Perpetual bulls. Perpetual bears.* But rarely are there professionals who truly see it coming. There is always a lot of denial—a rationalizing that something bad may be happening, but it's contained. The people who most often sense the danger aren't observing from the outside. They are living it.

For whatever reason, I seem to be one of those people. I always find myself embedded in the original source of stress before the full weight of a crisis is felt by the broader markets. In 2007, I had already been in the thick of the predatory mortgage environment. Not as an analyst, but as a casualty.

A Mortgage That Was Never Supposed to Exist

A year earlier, what I had hoped would be a major positive life event had turned into a nightmare. The mortgage I'd used to purchase my first home was improperly processed and ineligible for packaging and sale to Fannie Mae or Freddie Mac. My loan didn't qualify. My bank was stuck holding it. And so was I.

When I put my townhome on the market in the summer of 2007, I was forced to do so as a *short sale*—a scenario in which the property is worth less than the amount owed on it. To complete a short sale, the lender must approve the transaction, agreeing to accept less than the outstanding mortgage balance. My lender was Countrywide, then in the midst of its own collapse and being absorbed by Bank of America. Getting anyone to respond when offers were submitted proved nearly impossible. As the housing market and the mortgage-backed securities embedded in fixed-income portfolios everywhere began to melt down, I was one of the casualties.

The First Dominoes

Within my first three weeks at Russell, I found myself working alongside the team to manage multiple crises simultaneously. First, one of our credit managers, Sagecrest Capital, had halted redemptions, and we were among the investors subjected to those gates. Second, an unusual option income strategy had been pitched to us by another institutional hedge fund of funds, Fairfield Greenwich. We struggled to understand the underlying mechanics and quickly passed. The manager behind it was someone I'd never heard of: Bernie Madoff. Third, value stocks had begun a sudden, sharp decline not for fundamental reasons but because *margin calls* on less liquid securities like master limited partnerships (MLPs) were forcing indiscriminate selling.

While we were putting out fires, our colleagues managing more traditional investment strategies seemed entirely unbothered. While we watched liquidity evaporate in our corner of the investing universe, everyone else was certain it was contained and that they were insulated. They weren't observing what we were observing. They were nowhere near it.

The Day Bear Stearns Closed Its Doors

My time at Russell was short. As the holidays approached, our hedge fund of funds products came under severe duress. We had no choice but to *impose gates* of our own, suspending redemptions. Clients panicked. Before 2008 had even started, it was clear that the only viable path forward was an orderly liquidation of the funds. I called my dad and told him to move his retirement savings to cash. The worst was still coming.

On the day Bear Stearns closed its doors, I was summoned to a small conference room with five colleagues and told we were being let go. I was on the opposite coast from home, having relocated just months earlier, with no idea what came next. I was devastated and, strangely, unsurprised. I had watched it all unfolding. I had known.

Severance, Survival, and Starting Over

Russell was incredibly generous. Despite my short tenure, I received six months of salary and a full relocation package. Even so, I had no clear destination. Home to the East Coast felt like the only logical answer. I began applying for positions in Boston and New York City. If nothing came through, I'd simply move back in with my parents until I could get back on my feet.

I felt defeated. Just months from my 30th birthday, I was unemployed and about to be living in my childhood bedroom again. Everything I had built in Seattle—the career pivot, the new city, the sense of forward momentum—had been dismantled by forces larger than any of us.

Two Doors, One Decision

Thankfully, it wasn't long before two very different opportunities emerged. The first was my dream job: a research analyst role at MFS Investment Management, a well-established and highly regarded asset manager in the heart of downtown Boston, with a full suite of mutual funds and a name that carried real weight in the industry. The second was a research analyst position at a small, registered investment advisor in Waltham, Massachusetts, called Peak Financial. The role at Peak was markedly different. I would be responsible for evaluating investment managers for client portfolios, helping build in-house investment programs, and—most notably—exploring the development of an alternative investment capability.

As I packed my belongings for my second cross-country move in less than a year, I arrived at home with both offers in hand. On one side: the job I had dreamed about since the day I entered finance. On the other: a small, unknown firm managing individual client portfolios, with a nascent idea about alternatives that wasn't even fully formed yet.

Something told me Peak was the one. I had begun to fall deeply in love with the world of alternative investments, and I wasn't ready to leave it behind. I took the job at Peak. It turned out to be the best professional decision I ever made. It redirected the entire trajectory of my career in ways I couldn't have imagined at the time.

Gifts Are Hidden Inside Crises

The global financial crisis (GFC) was devastating for millions of people. It dismantled careers, wiped out savings, collapsed institutions, and shattered confidence in systems that most people had never thought to question. I was not spared. I lost my first home. I lost my job. I watched financial structures I had been hired to analyze begin to implode in real time.

And yet, I emerged from it better equipped to understand markets than I had been going in. Not because I read about it. Because I lived it.

That distinction matters more than most people realize. There is a difference between reading about the 2008 financial crisis and having been inside a hedge fund of funds when the first gates went up. There is a difference between understanding systemic risk as an academic concept and sitting in a conference room on the day Bear Stearns collapsed, learning you no longer have a job. Proximity to crisis is not something you would choose, but it changes how you see markets permanently. It teaches you things no textbook can replicate.

Here is what that experience forged in me and what it can teach you:

- The people closest to the problem always see it first. If you are embedded in an industry, a sector, or a system that is showing signs of stress, trust what you are experiencing even when the broader consensus tells you it is contained.
- Liquidity is everything. In calm markets, it is invisible. In crisis, it is the only thing that matters. An investment that cannot be sold when you need to sell it is not an investment; it is a trap.
- Prestige is not a strategy. I turned down what I had always considered my dream job. I chose a small, unknown firm over a household name because the work aligned with where I believed the opportunity was. That instinct proved right. Chasing a title or a brand at the expense of genuine conviction is how careers stagnate.

- Crisis accelerates clarity. The GFC forced me to identify, quickly and without sentimentality, what I actually knew, what I actually valued, and where I actually wanted to go. That kind of forced reckoning, as painful as it is, produces a level of self-knowledge that comfort never does.
- Recovery is not a return to the past. I didn't go back to the career I had before Russell. I went forward, into something new. The version of the financial industry that existed before 2008 was gone. The most important thing I could do was not mourn what had changed—but position myself inside what was emerging.

Alternative investments—hedge funds, private credit, real assets, noncorrelated strategies—were once the domain of institutional insiders and ultra-high-net-worth individuals. The GFC exposed how fragile the traditional 60/40 portfolio was when correlations collapsed and liquidity dried up. In the aftermath, the conversation about alternatives in client portfolios began to shift. I had been inside that conversation at exactly the right moment, learning the language, understanding the risks, and beginning to see the possibilities.

If the Queen of Alternatives began taking shape in 2007, by 2008 she was starting to build her empire. Not because the path was easy. Because the disruption was real and she had been standing close enough to feel it.

That is the lesson I want you to carry forward: your proximity to difficulty is not a liability. It is your most valuable form of market intelligence. The investors and professionals who emerge from periods of upheaval with the clearest vision are almost never the ones who watched from a safe distance. They are the ones who were in the room.

Chapter 13

Lights, Camera, Action: A Star Is Born

Wired for the Spotlight

Have you ever watched young children perform in front of an audience? Even at a very young age, it's easy to spot the child who lives for the stage and the one who would rather be anywhere else. Loving the spotlight, embracing an audience, excelling under pressure in front of a crowd, these are the exception, not the rule.

We are hardwired to avoid it. The same lizard brain that kept early humans alive viewed the spotlight as a threat. In early human societies, drawing attention to yourself was dangerous. Audiences didn't gather to celebrate. They gathered to watch what happened to people who stepped out of line. The stage was a place of consequence. Modern society has changed the setting. Most people, however, still fear the judgment that comes with being seen. A rare few seek it out.

I am one of those people.

For as long as I can remember, I wanted to perform. I sang and danced for my stuffed animals as a child. I loved dancing, acting, and the camera. It was this love of the spotlight that led me to modeling and pageantry. Not out of ego, but because performing feeds my soul in ways I have never been able to fully explain. It simply does. And when I accepted the job at Peak Financial, I had absolutely no idea that this quality, the one that had seemed entirely separate from my professional life, would turn out to be the most valuable skill I brought through the door.

The Hand No One Else Would Raise

When I joined Peak, the firm's founder, Pran Tiku, had just published his first book, *Six Sizzling Markets,* focused on the investment case for *emerging markets.* As part of the promotional effort, he had retained a PR firm, Gregory FCA, which quickly identified an opportunity to broaden not just awareness of the book but the firm's profile altogether.

The timing could not have been better or more chaotic. The financial crisis was still unfolding. The collapse of Bear Stearns had rattled markets, but full-scale panic had not yet set in. Demand for credible voices who could explain what was happening was enormous. Media outlets were hungry for compelling experts who could speak fluently about the economy, markets, and what came next. And the industry was eager to replicate the success CNBC had found with Maria Bartiromo—the original "money honey"—proof that women who could talk markets commanded real audience attention.

Gregory FCA suggested that Pran identify someone from the team to complement his media contributions. He would be the emerging markets voice. Someone else needed to cover everything else. He asked the team if anyone was interested. Being the newest member, I waited to see if a more senior colleague would step forward. No one did. The firm's portfolio manager made it explicitly clear: she had no interest in the spotlight. Once it was apparent that no one was going to volunteer, I raised my hand.

I had spent years developing extemporaneous speaking skills through pageantry, the ability to take an unexpected question and deliver a thoughtful, confident, articulate answer in real time. It is not a common skill. It turns out it is also exactly what live financial television requires.

August 7, 2008: The First Appearance

My very first media appearance was on CNBC's *Halftime Report* on August 7, 2008. I appeared alongside John Massey, senior portfolio manager at AIG SunAmerica. The S&P 500 was trading at 1,278. The Dow was at 11,541. The NASDAQ sat at 2,375. The conversation centered on how oil prices—then at $120 per barrel—were influencing investor sentiment. The 10-year Treasury was yielding 4%, which at the time was considered quite low.

Looking back at that appearance, two things strike me. First, how much has changed. Second, how much hasn't. The same core anxiety was present then that drives markets today: energy prices, interest rates, and the question of whether the system is fundamentally stable or quietly cracking. In August 2008, Bear Stearns had already collapsed, but the consensus was that it had been a speed bump, not a warning. That consensus was about to be shattered.

The Weekend That Changed Everything

On Friday, September 12, 2008, the rumors were already spreading: Lehman Brothers was in serious trouble. The Federal Reserve Bank of New York had called an emergency meeting to assess what a potential collapse might mean for the broader financial system. Lehman was a major investment bank. Its failure would send shockwaves through every corner of the markets.

That afternoon, I joined a special webinar hosted by a well-known fixed-income manager who expressed confidence that Lehman would survive. Bank of America and Barclays were both reportedly competing to acquire the firm, and the prevailing view was that a bidding war would produce a premium outcome. When markets closed that Friday, that sentiment appeared broadly shared.

The weekend told a different story entirely. The Treasury Department blocked the Bank of America deal. The Bank of England blocked the Barclays transaction. With no buyer and no rescue, Lehman Brothers filed for bankruptcy late Sunday afternoon. When markets opened Monday morning, they collapsed. The first domino—the real first domino—had finally fallen.

Finance Famous

Virtually overnight, everything changed. Suddenly every media outlet was desperate to secure a compelling voice to provide financial commentary. I went from being a complete unknown to a fixture on screens across New England. I appeared on morning news, evening news, and breaking coverage on WCVB-TV, the Boston area's ABC affiliate. I was featured regularly on NECN, the New England Cable News Network, not just in news segments but in longer-format evening programs where there was time to go deeper. I became a regular on *NewsNight* with Jim Braude. At one point, I was on television every single day. Reporters came to my home to film interviews. The *Wall Street Journal* was calling for quotes. Conference speaking requests flooded my inbox. Magazine features followed. And then came something I genuinely did not expect: fan mail. Real fan mail.

I joke that I am "finance famous"—a complete nobody in the wider world but something of a rock star within the industry. Autograph requests. Selfie requests. It was surreal, and in some ways still is. How did a small, unknown firm in Waltham, Massachusetts, produce a financial media presence that reached that level that quickly?

The answer is that the moment found someone who was ready for it. And I was determined not to let it pass.

The Gospel of Alternatives

I used the platform I had been handed to say something I genuinely believed. I wrote a white paper on the investment case for alternatives across all client portfolios. Not just for institutions or the ultra-wealthy but for everyday investors. It was received as a significant contribution to the wealth management conversation at the time. And it was rooted in something real.

While the markets were melting down, something quietly transformative was happening on the regulatory side. In 2007, the SEC had made a series of changes to the Investment Company Act of 1940—commonly known as the "40 Act"—which governs how mutual funds are structured and what they are permitted to invest in. Specifically, the SEC relaxed the leverage restrictions on registered funds. At the very moment that excess leverage was driving the crisis, regulators were opening a door that would ultimately give everyday investors access to strategies that had previously been available only to institutions and the ultra-wealthy.

Suddenly, *130/30* and *120/20 mutual funds* were entering the mainstream. That was interesting. But what truly excited me was something more fundamental: the strategies I had been studying at Russell, the hedge fund approaches I had learned to evaluate, decompose, and apply, could now be deployed in client portfolios through registered vehicles. The alternative investment program I had imagined when I joined Peak was no longer a vision. It was real.

I began building alternative allocations for Peak's clients during the height of the crisis. They not only helped clients navigate the volatility, but they also outperformed. Significantly. I felt like I had found something others hadn't yet seen, and I couldn't stop talking about it. Just as 529 College Savings plans had been my edge early in my career as a financial advisor—a corner of the market that others overlooked—being early to recognize that *alternative investments* were about to change the game entirely propelled my career to levels I had never anticipated. Before it was fashionable, I was preaching the gospel of alternatives. I have never stopped.

What the Spotlight Teaches

The story of this chapter is personal—but the investing lesson embedded in it is one of the most important principles I know: information asymmetry is the foundation of every great investment thesis, and the people who hold it almost never look like the ones you'd expect.

While financial media was consumed with the drama of Lehman's collapse and the daily cascade of market losses, a small regulatory change that had occurred a year earlier was quietly rewriting the rules of what everyday investors could access. The 2007 amendments to the 40 Act were not front-page news. They were not discussed on the programs I was appearing on. They were not part of the consensus narrative about what the crisis meant or where markets were headed. They were, however, among the most consequential structural shifts in the democratization of investing in a generation, and almost no one was paying attention.

That gap between what is happening and what is being talked about is where investment edge lives.

Here is what this chapter is really teaching:

- Regulatory change is one of the most underappreciated drivers of investment opportunity. When the rules governing what can be built, sold, or accessed shift—even quietly, even in dense legislative language—markets reorganize around the new reality. The investors who read those changes early, understand their implications, and position accordingly almost always have an advantage over those who wait for the trend to become obvious.

- The consensus is always behind. During the height of the GFC, the dominant narrative was destruction: what was failing, what had been lost, what could no longer be trusted. That narrative was not wrong—but it was incomplete. Underneath the collapse, new structures were forming. New vehicles were being legalized. New strategies were becoming accessible. The investors who were asking "what is being built right now?"—rather than only "what is falling apart?"—were the ones who positioned themselves for the decade of outperformance that followed.
- Access is an asset class. For most of its history, alternative investing was structurally unavailable to the majority of investors—not because the strategies were too risky but because the legal and regulatory frameworks excluded them. When those frameworks changed, it created a genuine democratization of return potential. Understanding which investor populations are gaining access to strategies they previously couldn't touch—and getting there first—is itself a form of alpha.
- Crisis is a stress test that reveals what actually works. The alternative allocations I built for Peak's clients during the GFC didn't just survive the volatility—they outperformed because the strategies were designed to behave differently from traditional equity and fixed-income exposures. That is the entire point of alternatives in a portfolio: not to eliminate risk but to introduce non-correlated return streams that hold up when conventional assets don't. The crisis didn't create that value. It exposed it. The best time to understand whether a strategy does what it claims is when markets are under genuine stress—not when everything is working.

- Being early requires being willing to look wrong. In 2008, talking about the investment case for alternatives—at the precise moment that hedge funds and complex structured products were being blamed for the collapse—was not a popular position. The instinct of most investors was to retreat to simplicity, to flee anything that seemed opaque or leveraged or unfamiliar. I was arguing the opposite: that what had failed was not the existence of alternative strategies but the misuse of them—and that the right application of those strategies was exactly what most portfolios were missing. Being early to a contrarian thesis is uncomfortable. It is also where the most durable returns are found.

The deeper principle here is one that runs through every chapter of this book: *the investors who build lasting insight are the ones who are embedded in the reality of markets—not just observing them from the outside but living inside the systems, the regulatory shifts, the structural changes, and the moments of dislocation that most people experience only as headlines.*

I was in the room when the first hedge fund gates went up. I was reading the regulatory filings when the 40 Act changed. I was on television explaining the crisis in real time, which forced me to synthesize what was happening with a clarity that purely internal analysis rarely demands. Each of those experiences sharpened my understanding of how markets actually function under pressure and what that means for where opportunity goes next.

That is what the spotlight taught me about investing. Not visibility for its own sake—but the discipline of translating complexity into clarity, in public, under pressure, when it matters most. That discipline, applied to research and portfolio construction, is what separates investors who understand markets from those who simply participate in them.

Chapter 14

After the Lights Fade: Love, Disruption, and the Markets That Test Your Conviction

The Lord's Work

My media success and the profile I had built at Peak Financial confirmed something I had long suspected: I had something real to contribute to the conversation about markets. But it also clarified something I hadn't fully reckoned with. There was a significant part of the role I didn't love. Dealing with clients.

It wasn't the clients themselves that were the problem. It was the nature of the interactions, particularly during a crisis. I often say financial advisors do the Lord's work, and I mean that sincerely. At its core, the role is part relationship management and part emotional counsel. Unlike institutions, individual investors have a deeply personal relationship with their money. They have life goals attached to it and dreams that depend on it. When markets dislocate, losses don't register as abstractions. They register as threats to the future they've been building toward. Fear and panic follow almost immediately.

As an investor, I have always been able to stay unemotional when managing other people's capital. And yet even I am not entirely immune. My own relationship with money has always been shaped by scarcity, by the bone-deep sense that it can disappear in the blink of an eye. I know what the right decision is. I also know how hard it is to make it when the stakes feel existential. During the financial crisis, I spent an enormous amount of time talking clients off the ledge. What I hadn't anticipated was that I'd eventually be doing the same for my colleagues.

The Call That Came from Chicago

The last week of February 2009, I left the office to attend a conference in Chicago. The week before my departure, I had walked our investment committee through a significant set of allocation changes I had made across all client portfolios. My read on the markets was clear: we were approaching the bottom. The moment called for conviction, not caution.

I shifted the portfolios from highly defensive to opportunistically positioned. I moved clients toward rock-bottom equity prices, increased overall equity risk, and built a targeted list of individual securities I believed were trading well below intrinsic value: Apple, Goldman Sachs, Ford, NVIDIA, and Amazon, among others. I rotated toward domestic U.S. growth managers, increased small cap exposure, and reduced Treasury holdings in favor of corporate credit and high yield. Within the alternatives bucket, I moved out of managed futures and into *master limited partnerships (MLPs)*, while adding a core position in distressed debt. When I left the office that Friday, the committee had agreed. I felt confident in the work.

I flew to Chicago Sunday evening, spent Monday at the conference, and was on my way to dinner with an old friend when my phone rang. It was the portfolio manager at Peak. She opened with three words that told me everything: "Shana, I tried." My stomach dropped. I knew exactly what came next.

While I was traveling, the team had convened without me. Despite the portfolio manager's objections, they had voted to abandon every change I had made and then gone further, shifting client allocations to an even more defensive posture than the one I had started from. I was livid. When I returned to the office, the models had been gutted.

One week later, on March 9, 2009, the market officially bottomed. Our clients were among the worst-positioned in the industry for the recovery that followed. By May, I was being blamed for the outcome.

I understood the dynamics at play. I didn't yet have the institutional track record that commands unquestioned authority. I knew I was a strong investor. But I also knew that being a young, attractive woman in this industry is an asset when the camera is on—and a liability when you're trying to be taken seriously in a conference room. It is a tension I have navigated my entire career and one that still invites unearned skepticism to this day.

Back to the Institutional World

I began my job search almost immediately. It didn't take long. Multiple offers came in from well-known firms that recognized what I brought to the table. By summer, I had accepted a senior investment associate position at Mercer—one of the world's leading investment consulting firms—and I was finally going to be managing multibillion-dollar institutional portfolios. It was the move I had been working toward for years.

What I hadn't fully considered was the trade-off. Mercer did not permit its investment professionals to work as outside media contributors. Overnight, I went from being a recognizable voice across New England's financial media landscape to another anonymous face in a building full of exceptionally talented investors. The spotlight I had stepped into so naturally simply. . .turned off.

The work at Mercer was serious and demanding in all the right ways. The team recognized my investment capabilities and moved quickly to give me opportunities intended to develop me toward a portfolio management role. I was managing institutional mutual funds for major firm clients. The intellectual challenge was exactly what I had been craving. The visibility was gone entirely. Both things were true at once.

The Facebook Message That Changed Everything

As my career settled into a more traditional trajectory, so too did the rhythms of my personal life. I was new at Mercer and hadn't yet accrued enough vacation time to join my family's annual trip to Disney World over April school vacation—a tradition my mom, a teacher, had maintained every year since I graduated college. My parents rented a large house with a pool and opened it up to everyone. I had gone every year without fail. That April, I couldn't go.

As it turned out, the universe had other plans for that weekend.

On a Saturday morning, I received a Facebook message from someone I barely knew. We had crossed paths briefly during my time at Morgan Stanley, but I wouldn't have called him an acquaintance. His name was Jason Sissel. He was in Boston for the marathon running with a small group to raise money for a charity he had founded called Endure to Cure (E2C). Following his grandfather's death, Jason had walked away from a lucrative investment banking career to build something that mattered to him. He lived in Chicago. He was only in town for a few days. Lunch, he suggested, seemed harmless enough.

I showed up late. Traffic into the city had been a nightmare. He waited anyway.

Lunch was easy and interesting. That evening, he invited me to join him for a Celtics game. I said yes. By the end of the night, he had made his intentions clear in a way no one had before: "You don't know it yet, but you're going to marry me."

He went back to Chicago. The pursuit did not slow down. He flew to Boston nearly every weekend. By June, he had packed a U-Haul and moved his entire life to be with me. It was a whirlwind. Before the year was out, he had proposed.

We married in September 2012 and began our life together in downtown Boston. I had by then returned to Fidelity, where my career was thriving. We were building something real.

The Day the Finish Line Became a Crime Scene

On the third anniversary of our first date—Patriots' Day, April 2013—I was at lunch a few blocks from the Boston Marathon finish line when the bombs went off.

The days that followed were strange and heavy. The city felt compressed. Police presence was everywhere. The air itself seemed different. Unlike my experience with 9/11, where I was young, far from home, and simply trying to survive the day, the Boston Marathon bombing found me in a different place in my life. I felt a pull not to retreat but to be present for the people around me who were struggling to process it.

The bombing clarified something. I was married. I was established. The next chapter of my life had a shape I could see: a home of our own, outside the city, and a family. Jason and I had been talking about it. The attack was the catalyst that turned the conversation into a plan. Sometimes it takes a moment of violent disruption to make you stop hesitating about the life you actually want to build.

When Being Right Is Not Enough

The investing lesson buried inside this chapter is one of the most uncomfortable ones in this book—because it has nothing to do with analysis and everything to do with human behavior.

In late February 2009, I made what turned out to be one of the most accurate market calls of my career. The bottom was days away. The portfolio repositioning I had designed—rotating into beaten-down equities, adding distressed debt, moving toward growth and away from defensive hiding places—was exactly right. The committee agreed. And then, when I was no longer in the room, they undid all of it.

The market bottomed on March 9, 2009. The recovery that followed was one of the great bull runs in modern market history. Our clients missed it. Not because the analysis was wrong, but because fear overrode conviction at the exact moment conviction was most required.

That experience taught me several things I have never forgotten:

- Emotion is the single greatest destroyer of investment returns. The academic research on this is unambiguous—investor behavior consistently underperforms the funds they invest in, because people buy high when confidence is abundant and sell low when fear takes over. The GFC was a masterclass in this dynamic. The investors who acted on logic at the bottom were rewarded. The ones who let panic drive the decision, even when the logical path had been clearly laid out in front of them, paid an enormous price.
- Being right too early is functionally the same as being wrong. Conviction without influence produces no outcome. This is a hard truth for anyone who prides themselves on analytical rigor. It is not enough to have the correct thesis. You must also be in a position where your thesis can be acted upon. That requires credibility, trust, and timing, none of which can be manufactured in the moment of crisis. They are built before the moment arrives.
- The bottom is always invisible until it has passed. No one rings a bell. The signals are there—valuations, credit spreads, sentiment extremes, the exhaustion of selling pressure—but they require interpretation under conditions of maximum

psychological stress. The investors who are able to act at the bottom are almost always the ones who have done the analytical work in advance and committed to a process that does not bend to fear. They are not braver than everyone else. They are more prepared.

- Institutional dynamics can be as irrational as individual behavior. One of the persistent myths in finance is that professional investors are immune to the emotional patterns that afflict retail participants. They are not. Committees defer to consensus. Consensus defers to the prevailing mood. In a crisis, the prevailing mood is almost always wrong at the extremes. The structure of group decision-making, designed to distribute risk and prevent rogue actors, can also suppress exactly the kind of independent conviction that generates outsized returns.
- Disruption, in markets and in life, forces clarity about what you actually believe. The Boston Marathon bombing did not change my investment philosophy. But it did remind me that time is finite, that the life you want to build does not assemble itself, and that hesitation has a cost. The same principle applies to every investment decision made in the shadow of uncertainty. Waiting for comfort is not a strategy. At some point, the analysis is complete, and the only remaining question is whether you are willing to act on what you know.

The market bottomed the week I returned from Chicago. The recovery that followed rewarded exactly the positions I had built and then watched be dismantled. I could not control the committee. I could not override the fear. What I could control was what I did next, how I channeled the frustration, where I took my conviction, and what kind of investor and professional I chose to become on the other side of being ignored.

That is ultimately the most important investing lesson this chapter has to offer. The market will not always validate your timing. The room will not always agree with your analysis. The people you are trying to protect will not always let you protect them. What you do in those moments, whether you abandon your process or deepen your commitment to it, determines the kind of investor you become over the long arc of a career.

The lights had faded. The spotlight was gone. The work, as always, was just beginning.

Chapter 15

Balancing Ambitions: Motherhood and the Woman's Career Journey

Living the Life I Had Worked For

In 2014, I was in the best place I had ever been. Jason and I had built a home in the Boston suburbs. I was thriving at Fidelity. I was as financially stable as I had ever been in my life, finally able to do the things I had spent years dreaming about from a distance.

Jason loved to travel, and for the first time I had the means to support those adventures. I had rediscovered horseback riding—a childhood passion I had set aside for years—and found my original instructor, Joe Lombard, teaching at his daughter's academy, Saddle Rowe, not far from our home. The life I had built was full in ways I hadn't known to expect. Jason poured himself into Endure to Cure and was building a travel blog as a way to monetize what he loved most. I was the primary breadwinner, the financial anchor of the household. I didn't mind. I was in a position to do it, and we were living well.

A Boy Named Gabriel

Motherhood was never something I felt a fierce, primal pull toward. At 36, I was pragmatic about it. My position was simple: if it happens, wonderful. But I wasn't going to chase it. No IVF. No egg freezing. No months of anxious hoping. If it was meant for me, it would come.

Jason felt differently. He was eager to become a father. So I agreed to give it a shot with the casual openness of someone who assumed it would take a while. Two weeks later, the test was positive.

I didn't react the way most people would. I hadn't had time to get comfortable with the idea. I had just signed a lease on a horse for the upcoming show season. I cried. Not from joy, but from the sudden, disorienting weight of a decision I hadn't fully made yet catching up with me all at once. It took a few weeks before excitement arrived.

But when it did, I knew certain things with complete clarity. I was going to have a boy. I had always known I couldn't handle a little version of myself, and my family had a heavy imbalance of girls. A boy felt right. I also knew his name: Gabriel. It took some convincing, but Jason eventually came around. From the moment I was ready to be a mother, I was ready to be Gabriel's mother specifically.

The Winter That Tested Everything

My pregnancy was not what I had imagined. I discovered I was expecting in October. As we moved toward the end of the year, Jason and I began planning for what a baby would mean financially. He understood that he would need to contribute more to maintain our life together. A local diving school had offered him the opportunity to work as an instructor if he could complete his certification—a process that required six weeks in Bonaire. He was a certified rescue diver and needed his Divemaster certification as the bridge to instructor status. In December, he asked if I'd support him spending February in Bonaire to complete the coursework. I was fully on board. The timing felt manageable. He'd be back before the hardest months of the pregnancy.

What neither of us could have anticipated was the winter of 2015. The Boston area was buried under more than 10 feet of snow between late January and the end of February, one of the worst winters on record. The transit system collapsed. Parking lots became snow farms. Fidelity shifted employees to remote work. I spent the worst weeks alone, working from home, visibly pregnant, without Jason, without my routine, without the structure that had always anchored me.

Jason returned after the storm passed. Two weeks later, my dog, Brady, was diagnosed with lymphoma.

The isolation of remote work, the physical demands of a difficult pregnancy, and the grief of watching my dog decline all hit simultaneously. I gained far more weight than expected—more than anyone could explain. Gabriel had settled on my sciatic nerve, and I was in near-constant pain. My performance at work, once a source of pride and momentum, began to slip. I was no longer the rising star I had been. I was someone just trying to get through the day.

I was forced to put my dog down one month before Gabriel was due. A week later, I went into premature labor during a portfolio manager meeting and had to rush myself to the hospital. The stress had spread into our marriage as well. Jason and I found ourselves in near-constant conflict. I spent the last three weeks of my pregnancy on bed rest, unable to keep food down. When my water broke two weeks before my due date, I felt only relief.

Gabriel

He was an absolute joy from the moment he arrived. I am profoundly grateful that I was given the most extraordinary son—the happiest, easiest baby I could have imagined. Whatever I had been through to get there was worth it. Completely and without reservation.

But the demands of a newborn are indifferent to professional ambition. Sleep deprivation is not a condition that makes nuanced investment decisions easier. My career began to suffer in ways I hadn't anticipated and couldn't fully control. At the same time, Jason was deeply unhappy being so far from his family in Iowa. After weighing everything, it became clear that the right move for Gabriel, for our family, was to move west.

Ariel Investments had been recruiting me for months. Chicago made sense. One week after we celebrated Gabriel's first birthday, we loaded a moving truck and drove 1,400 miles west, leaving behind the house we had built, the family I had been near my entire life, and the city where I had become who I was. Weekly family dinners became two or three visits a year. I knew what I was giving up. My son's well-being was worth it.

The Weight of Holding Everything

Motherhood is hard for everyone. For me, it arrived inside a particular configuration of pressures that compounded in ways I was not prepared for. I was a senior executive at a legendary investment firm led by one of the most accomplished women in finance. I was the primary financial provider for my household. I was a mother to a toddler in a city where I had no close friends and no family within reach. I had no outlet. No one to call at the end of a hard day who could actually show up.

The weight was immense. Conflict over finances became a fixture of our marriage. The constant tension between work obligations and the demands of being present as a mother meant that someone was always feeling neglected—and I was usually the one absorbing the guilt from both directions. Jason was focused on building his travel platform and raising Endure to Cure's profile. When he traveled or ran events, I couldn't join him. The distance between us widened.

2018 was the breaking point. I was let go from Ariel. For the first time in my professional life, I was not in a position to support the household financially. My job search lasted seven months—far longer than I had ever experienced—and drained the savings we had built. My mental health took a serious toll. Jason wasn't ready to set aside his ambitions. Everything was under strain.

I eventually accepted a position at CLS Investments, the investment arm of Orion Advisor Technology. It paid significantly less than I had been earning. But it was a strong team, a genuine learning environment, and—crucially—it put me back in the spotlight. Back in the world of alternatives. Back in front of financial advisors. It set the foundation for what would come next.

When I was hired, my manager Rusty Vanneman gave me a single piece of advice: "You have the opportunity to really build your personal brand, Shana. Embrace it. Become a household name. You are a star." It is the best, most life-changing professional guidance I have ever received.

Your Turn: The Advice That Changed Your Direction

Think about the most significant piece of advice you have ever received. Not the most expected or the most conventional, but the one that actually redirected something. The one that arrived at the right moment from the right person and landed differently than advice usually does. Who gave it to you? Were you in a position to receive it, or did it take time before you understood what they were really saying? And perhaps most importantly, did you act on it immediately, or did you let it sit until circumstance finally forced your hand? Rusty's advice to build my brand and own my platform

(continued)

(continued)

changed the entire trajectory of what came next, but it worked only because the years of unglamorous work that preceded it had created the foundation for it to mean something. The best advice is rarely generic. It is specific to who you are, delivered by someone who sees you clearly, at a moment when you are finally ready to hear it. If you have received that kind of advice and not yet acted on it fully, it is worth asking yourself what is still in the way.

Portfolio Management Is Personal Management

This chapter is one of the most personal in the book. It is also, in ways that are easy to miss, one of the most instructive ones about investing.

The events of these years—the pregnancy, the brutal winter, Jason's absence, the dog, the premature labor, the move, the job loss, the seven-month search—were not market events. But they produced something that every serious investor eventually has to reckon with: the recognition that your capacity to think clearly, act rationally, and execute with discipline is not static. It is directly affected by the conditions of your life.

Most investment frameworks treat the investor as a fixed variable, a rational actor who processes information and makes optimal decisions. The research on behavioral finance has spent decades dismantling that assumption in the context of markets. What gets discussed far less is how the circumstances of an investor's personal life affect their judgment, not just their emotional state in a given moment but their sustained capacity to think well over time.

Here is what these years taught me about that:

- Cognitive bandwidth is finite, and life competes for it. During the worst of 2015, I was managing grief, physical pain, professional pressure, and isolation simultaneously. My investment instincts were sound, but my ability to execute at the highest level was compromised. This is not a personal failing. It is a condition of being human. The most self-aware investors understand when they are operating at reduced capacity and adjust their risk accordingly. Doubling down during a period of personal chaos is the same category of error as doubling down in a market you don't fully understand. The conditions matter.
- Concentrating risk in any single income source is as dangerous personally as it is in a portfolio. For the better part of a decade, I was the sole financial support of my household. My income was the entire portfolio. When that income disappeared in 2018, there was no diversification to absorb the shock. The same principle that governs prudent portfolio construction—don't allow any single position to represent existential risk—applies with equal force to the financial architecture of a life. Building personal financial resilience is not a luxury. It is a structural requirement.
- Career disruption is a form of forced portfolio rebalancing. Losing my job at Ariel was devastating in the short term. It was also the event that redirected me toward CLS, toward the advisor channel, toward the technology intersection that would eventually become the foundation of Banríon, the capital management firm that I founded. Forced transitions, in portfolios and in careers, often produce outcomes that deliberate, comfortable

choices never would have. The question is not whether disruption will happen. It is whether you can resist the instinct to reconstruct exactly what you had before and instead ask what the new landscape actually makes possible.

- The most durable competitive advantages are the ones that compound quietly across the worst periods. I never stopped learning during those years. I was building expertise in the advisor space, in financial technology, in alternative investment product development at a time when my personal life was under maximum strain. None of it felt like strategic positioning in the moment. It was simply what I did because it was what I knew. That sustained intellectual engagement, maintained through conditions that would have caused many people to simply hold on and wait for things to improve, is what allowed the next chapter to move as quickly as it did.
- Knowing what you are building toward changes how you endure the difficult periods. *One of the hallmarks of a long-term investor is the ability to hold through volatility without abandoning the original thesis.* That capacity comes not from certainty about timing but from clarity about direction. In 2018, I did not know what came next. But I knew, without hesitation, who I was and what I was capable of. That knowledge—about your own investment in yourself—is what allows you to remain a buyer of your own future when the price feels impossibly low.

The piece of advice Rusty gave me on my first day at CLS—embrace your platform, become a household name, you are a star—landed the way it did because I had already paid for it. Years of building expertise in obscurity, of being underestimated, of doing the work without the recognition, had created the foundation that advice could actually build on. Visibility without substance is noise. Substance without visibility is waste. The two together, at the right moment, with the right direction, are how something lasting gets built.

That is the investing lesson this chapter is really about, not a specific trade or a sector call or a framework for evaluating alternatives. It is about the investor behind the portfolio. The human being who carries the strategy through years of compounding difficulty, makes mistakes, absorbs losses, holds convictions that feel lonely, and eventually emerges on the other side with something that could not have been built any other way.

Building wealth—in markets or in life—is not a function of avoiding hard years. It is a function of what you do inside them.

Chapter 16

Exit Strategy: The Hardest Trade I Ever Made

What I Grew Up Believing

In my family, divorce is not something that happens. My parents have been married for nearly 50 years and are still, genuinely, head over heels in love. Even through the hardest stretches, they were a team. Committed. Present. The same is true of nearly every member of my extended family. For most of my life, I was surrounded by people who had found their person and knew it. Who had built something that endured not because it was easy, but because they had both decided it would.

That was what I wanted. That was what I believed marriage was supposed to be. That belief, held as tightly as I held it, became both my greatest strength and my greatest liability.

If I'm honest with myself, I think I always knew Jason wasn't my soulmate. The man who had held that place in my life was Joe, and Joe had broken my heart into a thousand pieces in 2007. That kind of loss doesn't just hurt. It reshapes what you go looking for next. I found in Jason something I had wanted desperately: a man who pursued me without ambiguity, who declared his intentions early, who made the choice to be with me feel uncomplicated. I confused the relief of being chosen for the rightness of the choice.

The Marriage I Tried to Save

The cracks appeared before Gabriel was born. Looking back, the signs were there earlier than that. I simply was not willing to read them as what they were. Pregnancy changed things in ways I hadn't anticipated and couldn't fully explain to people who weren't inside it. What I can say is that the person I had married and the person who showed up during those months were not the same. I spent years trying to reconcile that gap.

I pushed for counseling. I pushed for Chicago. I restructured our life more than once, looking for the configuration that would allow us to become the family I had envisioned. Our counselor, after six months, reflected something back to me that I had been resisting: the will to save a marriage has to exist on both sides. I could not supply it for both of us.

What I want to be honest about is my own responsibility in the failure of the marriage and for how long I stayed. I am someone who does not quit. I believe in honoring commitments. I believe that difficulty is part of the process, not a reason to leave. Those are values I am proud of, yet in this chapter of my life, they worked against me. I held on because leaving felt like failure. Because I had grown up believing that the people I came from did not walk away from their marriages. Because I wanted Gabriel to grow up in the home I had. What I did not fully reckon with, for too long, was what it cost him—and me—to stay.

Without Jason there would be no Gabriel. That is a truth I hold without ambivalence. A life without my son is not something I am capable of imagining. But the decision to remain in a marriage long after it had stopped being healthy—for me, for Jason, and by extension for the child watching everything—is something I carry with real accountability. I chose to stay. I made that choice repeatedly. Understanding why I made it, and what it cost, is part of how I became who I am now.

2020: When Everything Broke at Once

By 2018 we had reached a breaking point. I was on the edge of a mental breakdown. I was not the mother Gabriel deserved, and I knew it. My stubbornness and my terror of what leaving would mean were the honest reason the marriage didn't end then. Travel, for both of us, created just enough physical distance to make what we were living feel survivable. It wasn't a marriage anymore. It was an arrangement I didn't yet have the courage to name.

Then 2020 arrived, and with it, nowhere left to hide.

The year had begun with real momentum professionally. I was thriving. Media appearances, speaking invitations, a recent promotion, a team of analysts. My role at Orion had moved to the center of the firm's transformation into a national brand. The portfolios I managed were top performers. I was deep in the work of rebuilding the firm's *turnkey asset management program (TAMP)* into an industry-leading solution. For the first time in years, I felt like I was exactly where I was supposed to be professionally, even as everything at home was coming apart.

Then the world shut down.

The state of Illinois issued its stay-at-home order on Friday, March 20. At nine o'clock Monday morning, my phone rang. It was Rusty. The firm had made the decision to put the TAMP business on hold. In a world turned upside down, my position was not mission critical. I was being let go.

I hung up in complete shock. The world was in freefall, I was now unemployed, and I was locked inside a home that had slowly become the loneliest place I had ever lived. In 2018, when I was laid off from Ariel, we had savings to absorb the blow. In March 2020 there was no cushion, no stability, and no version of staying that I could any longer justify to myself. I was 42 years old. I was in the darkest mental place I had ever occupied. And I was finally, irreversibly, done.

The Brand That Caught Me

In the wreckage of that week, I came back to something. The advice Rusty had given me on my first day at Orion: build your brand, embrace it, become a household name. I had done the work. I had invested in visibility with the same intentionality I brought to portfolio construction—consistently, over years, without knowing exactly when or how it would pay off. I had a large and genuinely engaged professional following. I had industry credibility. People knew my name and trusted my voice.

In the worst professional moment of my life, that brand was the net that caught me.

Within one week of my layoff, I had a new job. A better job. The title I had been working toward for years: chief investment officer. Spotlight Asset Group was a fast-growing registered investment advisor (RIA) aggregator, a firm that acquires independent wealth management practices and provides centralized infrastructure to support their growth. I would oversee all model portfolio offerings for the firm's advisor network and build an in-house alternative investment program from the ground up. I was also given the freedom to engage a PR firm and use my media profile to bring the firm's brand to a national audience. It was, in almost every dimension, the role I would have designed for myself.

As COVID restrictions began to lift and the world found its footing again, I found mine. I left on what would have been our eighth wedding anniversary. I took my son, I took nothing I didn't need, and I did not look back.

Cutting Your Losses

Every serious investor knows the hardest decision in portfolio management is not where to invest. It is when to exit. Knowing when a position that was right at entry is no longer right to hold—and having the discipline to act on that knowledge rather than the weight of what you've already committed—is one of the rarest and most consequential skills in investing.

This chapter is about that decision, lived out in the most personal context imaginable.

The cognitive patterns that cause investors to hold losing positions long past the point of rational justification are the same ones that can cause a person to remain in a situation long past the point where the original thesis is still intact. Understanding those patterns, in markets and in life, is how you develop the discipline to make better decisions in both.

Here is what this chapter teaches about investing:

- Sunk cost is the enemy of rational decision-making. The time, energy, and emotion you have already invested in a position are not relevant to whether it deserves continued capital. They are already spent. What matters is the forward-looking question: given what I know now, does this position deserve to remain in the portfolio? Investors who cannot separate what they have already paid from what something is currently worth will consistently hold losing positions longer than they should. The same is true wherever we allocate finite resources—time, trust, or capital.
- Hope is not a thesis. Wanting something to work is not evidence that it will. One of the most common errors in both investing and personal decision-making is mistaking emotional investment for analytical conviction. A thesis requires evidence. When the evidence no longer supports the original conclusion, the thesis must be revised regardless of how much you preferred the world in which it was still true. The longer you wait to make that revision, the more expensive the eventual exit becomes.

- The cost of holding is never zero. Investors sometimes treat inaction as a neutral choice. It is not. Holding a deteriorating position carries real costs: capital that cannot be redeployed, opportunity that is being missed, the ongoing drain of managing something that isn't working. Those costs compound quietly. By the time they are impossible to ignore, they have already done significant damage. Recognizing the cost of staying—before it becomes undeniable—is a discipline that has to be practiced deliberately.
- A forced exit can reveal an opportunity that a voluntary one never would. I did not choose to leave Orion. The decision was made for me. What I had, when the dust settled, was a brand built through years of consistent, unglamorous investment and that brand created options faster than any conventional job search could have. The position I landed was not something I would have pursued from a position of comfort. Disruption forced the reallocation, and the reallocation produced a better outcome. This is not a guarantee. But it is consistently true for investors, and people, who have been building something durable in the background, quietly, regardless of whether the current moment seems to reward it.
- Knowing your intrinsic value is not the same as accepting the market's current price for it. In 2020 I was 42 years old, unemployed, navigating a divorce, and in the darkest place I had ever been mentally. The market's momentary assessment of my situation bore no relationship to what I was actually worth or capable of. One of the most important disciplines an investor can develop—and one of the most important beliefs a person can hold about themselves—is the ability to distinguish between a temporary price and a permanent value. The market is wrong about individual securities all the time. It is also wrong about

people. Your job is not to accept the current quote as the final verdict. Your job is to know what something is actually worth and hold that knowledge even when nothing around you confirms it.

The day I accepted that my marriage was over was not the day I gave up. It was the day I stopped allocating further resources to a position that the evidence had long since stopped supporting and redirected that energy toward something with a real chance of compounding.

Cutting a loss is not the same as accepting failure. In investing, the ability to exit a deteriorating position—cleanly, without sentiment, without waiting for a recovery that isn't coming—is a mark of discipline, not defeat. It frees capital. It restores clarity. It creates the conditions for the next right decision.

The same is true in life. Some of the most important moves you will ever make will not look like progress in the moment. They will look like loss. The measure of the decision is not how it feels when you make it. It is what it makes possible afterward.

I left on our anniversary with my son and my clarity. That was enough. It turned out to be everything.

Chapter 17

A New Chapter: Single Motherhood, Lost Love, and Career Volatility

Starting Over, Again

Deciding to end my marriage was easy. Actually leaving was hard.

I had been the financial foundation of the household for years. What that meant in practice was that I had very little financial independence of my own. Since 2018 my earnings had declined while the household budget expanded. To keep the peace, I had made significant personal sacrifices—to my savings, to my credit—to maintain a status quo that was never sustainable. When the moment finally came to go, I didn't just need the courage to leave. I needed the money to build an entirely new life from nothing.

I emptied what remained of my savings to furnish a house that Gabriel could feel at home in. Plates. Silverware. Cookware. Furniture. All of it acquired with the same pragmatism I had always brought to difficult decisions. Budget everything. It didn't need to be beautiful; it needed to be ours. I was starting from scratch at 42, in the middle of a global pandemic, in a city I had moved to for a marriage that no longer existed. It was humbling in ways I hadn't anticipated and clarifying in ways I hadn't expected.

COVID, for all its devastation, offered one practical mercy: financial institutions were extending relief programs to customers under hardship. I took full advantage of everything available and kept my expenses stripped to what was genuinely necessary. The restrictions that had upended the world also created a kind of enforced simplicity that made rebuilding feel almost manageable.

Jason and I had agreed to 50/50 custody. My instinct had been to resist the weeks without Gabriel, but those stretches turned out to be exactly what I needed. Time to sleep. Time to think. Time to begin, slowly and without a roadmap, putting myself back together.

September 11, 2020

I was still finding my footing as a newly single mother when a notification appeared in my Facebook Messenger. A message request from a name I had not seen in 13 years.

Joe.

My stomach turned. I felt physically nauseated. I opened the message.

> *"Shana, it has been some time since we last communicated but wanted to reach out considering it is the eve of September 11th. There are only a handful of people who could understand what you and other survivors went through and endure. Having seen some of my friends go through traumatic events, I pray for your well-being and continued success. In just looking you up to connect, there is no doubt you have taken your experiences and forged forward an ambitious and variegated life. Inspirational is often a backneyed way to describe a modicum of achievement given the individual. Your story is nothing short of inspirational and*

I have no doubt your family and friends share your pain in being a survivor but also relish in your perseverance. Wishing you the best, Joe."

My Joe. THE Joe. The man who had shattered my heart into a thousand pieces 13 years earlier. The love of my life who had chosen someone else. The man I had spent more than a decade working to forget or at least convincing myself I had.

I had no idea what to do with it. We had had no contact since 2007. No mutual friends. No common professional world. He had been in the military and was based in Washington D.C., a city with virtually no overlap with the financial industry I inhabited. The timing did not feel accidental. It felt then, and still feels now, like the universe was doing something deliberate. I had filed for divorce just weeks earlier. And here, completely without warning, was the person I had never fully stopped loving.

I called my mom. Then my friend Penny. Then my closest friend from college, Kat. All three expressed the same reservations in their own ways. They reminded me how badly it had ended. They reminded me that he had made his choice in 2007 and it hadn't been me. Intellectually I understood every word of it. But something in me was already certain this was not a coincidence, and I could not pretend otherwise.

Before I responded, I went to my email archive and found the folder I had buried there years ago. The messages from 2007, from his wife. I needed to look at them again. I needed to remind myself of what that had cost me and to be honest with myself about whether what I was feeling was wisdom or just old longing dressed up as fate. I sat with that for 24 hours before I typed a single word back.

I kept my response neutral. Warm enough to acknowledge his message, careful enough not to invite anything further. It was enough.

His reply opened every door I had spent 13 years keeping shut.

"I think of you every year on the anniversary. How could I not? If I'm being honest I think about you way more than I should. I know I hurt you, I have never forgiven myself for how I hurt you, and I in no way think I deserve your forgiveness. I want you to know, I've never stopped thinking about you, about the decision I made. I thought it was the right one. It wasn't. Losing you was one of the biggest mistakes of my life and I've felt incomplete since that day. I hope you know that what we had was real. I hope you know I was young and dumb and didn't want to tie you down when you were meant to fly. It looks like that's what you've done. You're on TV, I watched your clips, I have no clue what you were talking about but. . .how are you still so smoking hot?"

Tampa

And so began the second act of a love story I thought was finished.

We messaged constantly. Inside jokes that had survived 13 years intact. Memories revisited without awkwardness. He had been divorced for years and was working through the end of a more recent relationship. He had a very young daughter he was absolutely smitten with, navigating the complexity of keeping her close while maintaining something workable with her mother. He had just transitioned from full-time military service into corporate life, thriving in it, genuinely happy to be wearing suits again, having them tailored to fit properly. He was still charming, funny, and sharper than ever. More handsome than I had allowed myself to remember.

It felt like 13 years had been 13 minutes.

In early December, he invited me to join him for part of an extended work trip to Tampa. Florida's restrictions were more relaxed than Illinois'. The idea of a few days of something approaching normalcy was appealing. I told him I needed to think about it and then called Penny immediately.

I had developed real confidence issues during my marriage. I had lived for years inside an environment that had quietly and persistently communicated that I was not enough. Not attractive enough, not desirable enough. That kind of sustained message does something to a person. It had done something to me. The thought of standing in front of Joe again—in real life, without the armor of a camera or a stage, was genuinely frightening. What if the chemistry was only nostalgia? What if he saw me clearly and the spell broke?

Penny told me to go. She also told me: "What if it's amazing, though? What if it's better than you remember?" I had not let myself consider that. I didn't want to set myself up for a fall; I wasn't sure I could survive again. But I went.

Penny was right. Tampa was nothing short of magical. Whatever I had been carrying—the years of suppression, the grief I had never fully processed, the part of myself that had gone quiet and stayed quiet—came back to life. I couldn't pretend anymore. I had never stopped loving him. I had simply needed to function without him, and I had mistaken that for being over it.

It was mutual. He was clear about that. He called me the one who got away. His person. His twin flame, and I say that fully aware of how that sounds, but I mean it precisely. Not soulmates in the conventional sense, but something rarer: two people who are mirrors for each other, who accelerate each other's growth in ways that can't quite be explained. Joe reminded me immediately who I was. The woman who had gone quiet inside an exhausting life reappeared. My eyes, which had been dull for longer than I wanted to admit, started to sparkle again. He breathed something back into me that I hadn't realized I was missing. Everything—at home, at work, with Gabriel, with myself—felt more alive because of it.

The Dream Life

Professionally, 2021 was everything I had worked for.

I was thriving as CIO of Spotlight Asset Group. My boss Steve and I aligned in our vision for the firm. He also understood the life I was navigating, a divorced single parent himself, and gave me room to excel rather than just perform. He pushed me further into the spotlight rather than pulling me back from it. I became a daily presence on Fox Business. CNBC was calling. Awards and magazine features arrived with a regularity that still felt surreal. I was living, in the most literal sense, the professional life I had been working toward since I first walked into Morgan Stanley Dean Witter in Worcester, Massachusetts, and decided I belonged somewhere bigger.

Joe proposed that summer. I wanted to say yes with everything I had. The divorce wasn't final yet. COVID had slowed the proceedings in ways neither Jason nor I had anticipated or wanted. There was nothing contentious between us: 50/50 custody, no shared assets, finances that had never been formally combined. The delays were procedural, not personal. But I was also aware of how things looked from the outside. I had moved on quickly, to someone with whom I had a long and documented history. People talked. I didn't want to disrespect the father of my son, or my son himself, with optics that could have been avoided. I told Joe we would have to wait. He understood.

The summer of 2021 was one of the most extraordinary of my life. Professionally fulfilled, personally restored, a son who was thriving, a love that felt like it had finally arrived at the right time. It was the life I had always believed was possible.

October

It ended in October 2021 without warning.

Spotlight experienced a sudden and severe operational disruption. Advisors left. Revenue and assets evaporated almost overnight. Steve fought hard to hold the firm together, but there was nothing to be done—he could not maintain his senior staff through what was unfolding. In a single month, the CIO, the COO, and the CCO all found themselves out of work. The dream life I had been living, the one that had arrived so fast and felt so right, was gone just as suddenly.

Reality landed hard. The runway I had built was shorter than it had appeared. And I was standing at the edge of it again.

The Risk You Stop Seeing When Everything Is Working

The investing lesson embedded in this chapter is one that most people only learn the hard way: the moment everything feels perfect is frequently the moment you are most exposed.

In 2021, I was not thinking about risk. I was thriving. The professional role was everything I had worked for. The personal life I had rebuilt felt like a reward finally arriving. Joe was back, the divorce was nearly done, Gabriel was flourishing. When all of your positions are working simultaneously, the natural human response is to stop stress-testing them. Optimism displaces vigilance. Confidence shades into complacency. And the vulnerabilities that were always there—in the firm, in the structure, in the dependencies you stopped examining—are still accumulating quietly in the background.

This is not a unique failure of judgment. It is a documented feature of how human beings process risk. Markets behave the same way. The conditions that produce the most spectacular collapses are almost always preceded by extended periods of calm—periods in which volatility is low, returns are strong, and the incentive to remain cautious feels increasingly unnecessary. The Lehman collapse, the dot-com implosion, the GFC: none of them arrived without warning signs that were visible in retrospect. What made them so destructive was that by the time they arrived, most participants had stopped looking.

Here is what this chapter teaches about investing:

- Concentration in a single source of income or return is always a risk, regardless of how strong that source appears. My entire professional existence in 2021 was dependent on a single firm, a single boss, and a single strategic direction. When the operational disruption hit Spotlight, there was no other position to absorb the impact. A diversified portfolio—of skills, of relationships, of income streams, of visibility—is not built as a precaution against success. It is built precisely because success creates the illusion that concentration is safe.
- Operational risk is the risk that gets ignored during bull markets. The collapse of Spotlight had nothing to do with my performance, my investment thesis, or the quality of the work I was doing. It was an operational failure—a structural breakdown in how the firm was run that had nothing to do with the market environment. Every investment, in every firm and every vehicle, carries operational risk alongside market risk. Evaluating only the strategy without evaluating the infrastructure that executes it is a form of incomplete due diligence. The most sophisticated investors treat operational risk as a first-order concern, not an afterthought.
- The assets that survive disruption are the ones you own outright. When Spotlight collapsed, I lost the role, the title, and the institutional platform. What I did not lose was the brand I had

built, the relationships I had cultivated, the expertise I had developed, and the reputation I had earned. Those assets were mine. They were not contingent on any single employer's continued existence. In investing terms: they were unencumbered. The effort I had put into building something portable. Following Rusty's advice—investing in visibility and credibility over years—was not just a career strategy. It was a form of personal asset allocation that paid off every time an external structure failed.

- Recovery speed is a function of preparation, not luck. I had been through enough disruptions by this point to understand something important: the investors and professionals who recover fastest from sudden dislocation are almost never the ones who happen to get lucky breaks. They are the ones who, in the periods of stability and success, kept building things that would matter when the stability ended. The personal brand. The network. The expertise that crosses firm boundaries. The financial discipline that creates even modest runway when income disappears. None of these feels urgent when everything is working. All of them become the deciding factor when it stops.
- The return of something lost is not the same as stability found. Joe's reappearance in my life was real and transformative; the joy it produced was not illusory. But the lesson embedded in the timing is worth naming: reconnecting with something that once brought tremendous meaning does not inoculate you against the other risks in your portfolio. The exhilaration of personal restoration can create the same blind spot that a strong bull market does, a sense that because one important thing is finally right, the others must be too. They are not correlated. Each position requires its own assessment, regardless of how good the overall portfolio feels.

October 2021 was not the end of anything. It was the beginning of something I could not yet see clearly from inside the shock of it. But what it taught me and what I want you to carry forward from it is that the most dangerous moment in any market, any career, or any life is not the obvious crisis. It is the period of apparent ease just before it.

Vigilance is not the enemy of joy. It is what allows joy to be sustainable. *The investors who build lasting wealth are the ones who never fully stop asking the question: what am I not seeing right now?* Not from fear, but from discipline. Not because they expect catastrophe, but because they understand that the absence of visible risk has never once meant the absence of actual risk.

The dream life was real. It was also, structurally, more fragile than it looked. That is not a reason not to build it. It is a reason to build it on foundations you actually own.

Chapter 18

One Big Leap: The Journey to Entrepreneurship

A Free Agent

Losing my job at Spotlight in October 2021 was jarring. It was also, strangely, not as destabilizing as it might have been. Joe was there. He was steady and certain in a way I hadn't experienced before—a partner who genuinely believed in what I was capable of, who would not allow me to spiral, who showed up in exactly the way I had always needed someone to show up. I do not underestimate the value of that. In moments of professional freefall, having someone beside you who sees you clearly and still has no doubt. That matters more than most people will admit.

Spotlight had also done something that couldn't be undone: it had elevated my profile to a level I hadn't previously reached. I was a recognized name in my industry, a regular face on national financial media, and a sought-after voice on alternative investing. When I became a free agent, my inbox filled quickly. Firms competed for my attention. I was negotiating from a position of genuine strength, and I knew it.

One of those conversations was with Mark Tepper, CEO of Strategic Wealth Partners (SWP). Mark had built SWP's national reputation largely through earned media; he understood its power in a way many firm leaders still didn't. He had been developing a young advisor at the firm for the spotlight and believed that adding a woman with my media profile would meaningfully complement what they were building. They also wanted to expand their alternatives offering, which placed me squarely at the center of their strategic priorities. I flew to Cleveland just before Halloween, negotiated the terms, and accepted the role. The search had lasted less than a month.

The Call on the Way to School Pickup

The structural challenge at SWP was one I didn't fully appreciate until I was inside it: I was the only remote employee. When you aren't physically present in an office every day, the invisible connective tissue of a workplace—the casual conversations, the trust built in hallways and conference rooms—doesn't form in the same way. It can't be manufactured through video calls. Shortly after I started, the entire staff tested positive for COVID, and the office shut down for three weeks. My first month was spent on a professional island. The second was fractured by the holidays. By January, the lack of real connection had made itself felt in ways I couldn't course correct.

In mid-January, I was a headline speaker at a Portfolio Summit event in Chicago. Two panels. A room full of peers and prospects. When I stepped off the stage that afternoon, I was surrounded; business cards were exchanged, follow-up conversations were promised. I had to leave to pick Gabriel up from school. I got in the car, merged onto the expressway, and my phone rang. It was SWP's COO.

"Shana, I'm sorry, but this just isn't working out. If you ship your laptop back by the end of the week, we'll pay you through month end."

By the time I reached Gabriel's school and checked my email, my access had already been cut. Every business card I had handed out that afternoon had my SWP contact information on it. All of it was already useless.

I sat in the school parking lot trying to understand what had just happened. I had barely gotten started. How was I back here again?

Why Don't You Just Start Your Own Firm?

This time, the offers did not come in fast. Losing a job once is understandable. Being let go two-and-a-half months after being hired is a different kind of signal. One that the market reads in a particular way, regardless of the actual circumstances. The conversations slowed. People who had been enthusiastic became cautious. I understood why. From the outside, the pattern was visible in a way that the full context wasn't.

Joe asked me why I didn't simply start my own firm. It wasn't the first time I'd heard the question—Jason had asked the same thing more than once during our marriage. My answer had always been identical: I don't have the pedigree, and I don't have the capital. The pedigree argument no longer held. The capital argument still did. My financial position was precarious. The divorce had been expensive—I had absorbed essentially all of it. My savings had never had a real chance to rebuild after 2018. The idea of adding entrepreneurial uncertainty to an already unstable situation, with a son whose stability was my first obligation, was not a risk I was willing to take.

A friend helped me find a short-term consulting engagement to bridge the gap while I searched. By March I had two substantive offers. The first was a high-profile role as Director of Alternatives at one of the largest RIA firms in the country, a big position at a recognized institution, with significant travel requirements. The second was Director of Investments at a small family office in Washington D.C. called Cope Corrales.

The Cope Corrales role had a particular kind of gravity to it. They had originally envisioned a CIO position but had two strong candidates and ultimately split the responsibilities, offering him the CIO title and creating the Director of Investments role for me. Under ordinary circumstances that distinction might have given me pause. Under these circumstances, the geography made the decision feel almost predetermined: 10 days a month in D.C., where Joe was, where our future was beginning to take shape, where he was buying a house and asking me to be part of that decision. I turned down the larger opportunity and accepted Cope Corrales.

Two Conversations That Broke Me Open

I had been at Cope Corrales for less than a month when Joe and I had our first serious argument about our future. He was working through the terms of a custody agreement for his daughter, a relationship and a situation with a great deal of complexity that is ultimately not my story to tell. What I can tell you is how it landed with me.

Joe was a devoted father. His sons were in Texas; his daughter was young and local, and he was determined to make sure she remained close. I understood that completely. Gabriel was my entire world. I never wanted to threaten what Joe had with his children. What I struggled with—what reawakened something old and unresolved in me—was the way the dynamics of that situation continued to give another woman a kind of presence in our relationship that I could not reconcile. I knew it was unfair. I knew the situation was genuinely complicated. But it felt, in the part of me that was still not entirely healed, like being not quite chosen. All over again.

I told him I couldn't keep waiting in that uncertainty. I stopped answering his calls. He gave me space. I knew he missed me. I missed him. But I didn't know how to hold both the love and the fear at the same time without one of them winning.

In early June 2022, the founders of Cope Corrales held a 90-day review call. For 30 minutes, they told me how exceptional my contributions had been—clients were thriving, portfolios were outperforming, colleagues had given glowing feedback. I was relieved and genuinely happy. I loved the work. I loved the balance of Chicago and D.C. I was exactly where I wanted to be.

At the end of those 30 minutes, they let me go. "Your contributions would be better suited for a larger firm."

The tears came before I could stop them. I asked if there was anything I could do. I reminded them that I had turned down another offer, a significant one, because they had assured me they were certain about this hire. They confirmed through email that my performance had been without fault. They simply felt I was meant for something bigger.

I had no framework for what had just happened. I still don't fully understand it. What I do know is its effect: three job losses in eight months made me radioactive in a way that had nothing to do with my actual record and everything to do with how the pattern looked. Long-term supporters went quiet. Interviews dried up. A year earlier I had been at the apex of my professional life. That summer, I was shopping for Instacart to keep the lights on.

The Queen of Alternatives Is Born

Joe and I reconciled that summer. It was not the effortless reunion that Tampa had been—there were things between us that needed more time and more honesty to work through. But by August we had found our footing again, and he asked me once more why I didn't just build something of my own.

I still had no capital. My bank account was empty. I had promised Gabriel a trip to Disney World in September and had no clear plan for how to pay for it. The gap between where I was and where starting a firm would require me to be seemed impossible to cross.

And then, with three weeks until Disney and nothing left to lose, I simply decided. I had been the person behind other people's platforms long enough. If everything I had built could be taken away this many times, it was time to build something that couldn't be.

Banríon was born.

My friend Cinthia invited me onto her firm's *Think Tanked* podcast to announce the launch. As we prepared for the recording, she asked about the name. I told her I had originally wanted Queen Capital—but it sounded flat, and it was already taken. So, I went to Google Translate and asked for the word "queen" in every language spoken in the world. As I read through the results, I was drawn immediately to the Irish Gaelic translation: Banríon. My mother was born in Ireland. The word had weight and music. Banríon Capital it was.

As we wrapped up the recording, Cinthia said it off-handedly, the way people say things they don't know will change everything: "Banríon means queen—which fits, since you're the Queen of Alts."

That was the moment. The Queen of Alternatives existed in an instant, and the response was immediate. Suddenly I wasn't another talking head with a title and a firm behind me. I was something with a name, a brand, an identity that belonged to no one but me. The business gained traction faster than I had dared to hope. As 2023 began, I had secured $450,000 in initial capital. All those years I had declined to take the leap—and it was from the absolute bottom that I finally built something real. This time, it was mine.

Building Something You Cannot Lose

This chapter is, in investing terms, the clearest possible illustration of why the assets you own outright—unconditionally, independent of any employer, any firm, any market cycle—are the ones that ultimately determine your floor.

In two years, I lost four jobs. Not because my work was poor. Not because my instincts were wrong. Because of operational failures, remote work dynamics, strategic pivots, and decisions made in rooms I wasn't in. Every single time, the thing that caught me was the same: a personal brand and a body of expertise that no one could take away when they ended my access and shipped my laptop back.

That asymmetry—between what is positional and what is portable—is one of the most important concepts in both investing and professional life. Here is what this chapter teaches:

- The most durable assets are the ones with no counterparty risk. A title, a salary, an institutional platform—these are real and valuable, but they are contingent. They exist at the pleasure of a decision made by someone else, in a room you may not be in. A brand, a reputation, a body of knowledge, a genuine network of people who trust your judgment: these carry no counterparty. When the firm closes, the access gets cut, the COO calls on the way to school pickup—none of that touches what you actually own. Building those assets deliberately, over years, regardless of whether the current institutional moment seems to reward it, is not a career strategy. It is a form of wealth creation.
- The bottom is where the most authentic businesses are built. Banríon was not launched from a position of confidence and abundant capital. It was launched from empty savings, a Disney trip to fund somehow, and the accumulated exhaustion of watching everything external get taken away. The companies built from genuine necessity—where the founder has nothing left to protect and no version of the status quo worth preserving—often carry a clarity of purpose that more comfortable launches do not. The question "what do I actually have to lose?" is one of the most clarifying questions an entrepreneur

or an investor can ask. When the answer is "very little," the calculus changes completely.

- Naming matters more than most investors realize. The moment "the Queen of Alternatives" existed as a phrase, everything shifted. Not because the underlying expertise or track record changed—those had been consistent for years. But because a name created an identity that was instantly legible, memorable, and differentiated in a market full of people with similar credentials. In investing terms: it was a brand premium applied to an already strong underlying asset. Investors consistently undervalue the role of narrative in creating and sustaining value. The best businesses, and the most enduring personal brands, are the ones whose story can be told in a sentence that no one else can claim.
- Repeated failure is data, not verdict. Four job losses in two years is a pattern that the market will read as disqualifying. It is also, viewed from the inside with full context, something else entirely: a sequence of structural and operational failures at firms that were themselves in various stages of instability, combined with a remote work dynamic that was genuinely unsuited to how trust and credibility are built inside organizations. The story the market tells about a pattern is not always the accurate one. The investors who build lasting portfolios and the founders who build lasting companies are the ones who can distinguish between a genuine failure of judgment and a run of external conditions that produced similar-looking outcomes. Self-awareness about the difference is not self-deception. It is due diligence applied to your own record.
- Timing the leap is less important than taking it. I had been told for years—by Joe, by Jason, by my own professional

instincts—that I had what it took to build something of my own. I had always found a rational reason to wait: not enough capital, not the right moment, too much at stake. The leap I finally took happened not because the conditions were right but because every other option had been exhausted. The firms I had trusted to hold my career had all, one by one, failed to do so. The only platform that had never once been taken from me was the one I had built myself. Sometimes the market forces the reallocation that prudent analysis should have recommended years earlier. The outcome is the same. The only question is how many opportunities you defer while waiting for certainty that was never going to arrive.

Banríon did not begin as a grand vision. It began as a name, a podcast appearance, and a phrase a friend said after someone pressed Record. What made it real was everything that had come before it—20 years of expertise, a hard-built reputation, a personal brand that had survived every institutional failure that tried to define me, and the willingness, finally, to put my name on something that no one else could take.

That is the investing principle at the center of this chapter: the highest conviction position you will ever hold is the one you take in yourself. Not because it is without risk, it carries enormous risk. But because when you have done the work, built the knowledge, survived the losses, and developed the judgment that only comes from having been tested repeatedly, you are, finally, an asset worth concentrating in.

The Queen of Alternatives was not born the day I started the firm. She was built across every chapter of this book. September 2022 was simply the day she stopped working for someone else.

Chapter 19

Dark Days: Confronting Loss and Mortality

What I Had Always Wanted

At the end of 2022, I knew—for the first time in a very long time—that I was doing exactly what I was meant to do.

People often assume that someone with my career trajectory must have always been reaching for the top. The corner office. The biggest title. The most prestigious firm. That was never the dream. My dream was simpler and more specific than that. Since I was a little girl, I had wanted to marry someone who truly loved me, buy a modest house in the suburbs, and have children, a dog, a cat, a reliable car, and the quiet assurance that the bills were paid. A vacation or two a year. Something nice occasionally. Not wealth. Comfort. Not a mansion. A home. Exactly what my parents had built.

Finance had expanded what I thought was possible. The last decade had shown me that the simple dream was harder to reach than I had expected, and the path toward it was rarely straight. But when Banríon launched and immediately found its footing, when my professional reputation grew faster than I could have planned, I felt something settle in me. The years of instability, the four job losses, and the grinding uncertainty had been pushing me toward this. The things that hadn't stuck hadn't stuck because they weren't what my life was meant for. This was.

Banríon continued to thrive in 2023. So did Gabriel.

Sensei Fonseca and the Competition Team

Gabriel had started training at a local karate dojo in late 2021. By the following year, he was ready to compete. In November 2022, he entered his first tournament, the Fonseca Cup, a premier international event organized by his own dojo. He had trained seriously. He had prepared with a focus and a discipline that was striking to watch in a seven-year-old. He could not wait to get on the mat.

It did not go the way he had hoped. Despite everything he had put in, he finished last in his division in both kata and kumite. He was devastated in the way only a child can be—fully, without any of the composure that adults learn to perform over grief. He sobbed, and I held him, and my heart broke for him quietly while I tried to hold steady on the outside. He told me he wanted to quit. I knew it wasn't the moment for a lecture about perseverance. I just let him feel it.

As we made our way toward the exit, the founder of the dojo—John Fonseca, the tournament's namesake—saw Gabriel crying and stopped us. He asked if he could have a moment with him. I had never formally met Sensei Fonseca. So, I sheepishly nodded and found a bench near the entrance doors and waited.

I have never asked either of them what was said in those 15 minutes. What I know is that Gabriel came running back to me with completely different eyes. "Mom, I want to join the competition team!"

I didn't know yet what that decision would mean for both of us. I would soon find out.

Orlando, December 2022

A few weeks later, I flew to Orlando. Joe had a work conference, and we had planned time together afterward, some breathing room in what had been a demanding few months for both of us. I don't know exactly how to describe the energy I felt when I saw him that first evening. It wasn't doubt about us. It was something stranger than that. An urgency I couldn't name. A feeling that I needed to be completely present, completely intentional, in a way I couldn't explain.

Before we went to sleep that night, I told him I loved him. But the way I said it wasn't casual. It felt like something I needed him to understand, not just hear. He seemed puzzled by the intensity of it. That feeling—the unnamed urgency—stayed with me for the rest of the trip.

On the last day, we were sitting at our departure gates, which happened to be right next to each other. I took a photo of us. We looked happy. Easy. Right. When his boarding group was called, I walked over and gave him one more goodbye. "I hope you know how much I love you, Joe. Truly. Deeply. Madly." He smiled, kissed me, and said he loved me too. I watched him walk toward the jetway.

It was the last time I saw him.

The Unraveling

Joe had started a new and significantly more demanding job in 2022. The role paid more and carried more weight, but it was exacting in ways that seemed to be wearing on him. I invited him to join me in Miami Beach for a speaking engagement in early 2023. A beautiful suite, ocean views, time carved out for just the two of us. He said yes and then changed his mind a week before. I invited him again in May for another conference. He said yes again. Then, in late April, he backed out a second time.

I was angry. It had been five months since Orlando. It was the longest stretch without seeing each other since we'd reconnected. When he told me he wasn't coming to Miami, I pressed him. He cited the PhD program he had started in late 2022. I didn't accept it as an explanation. A year earlier we had been looking at houses together, chosen a ring, talked in concrete terms about our future. Now he couldn't find a weekend.

The conversation became an argument. I told him he was doing what he had always done; keeping me at arm's length, making me feel like I was almost chosen but never quite. That landed hard. He called me needy. He said he was exhausted by having to constantly reassure me. He said it was unattractive. I was stunned. In 25 years—through every difficult stretch, every painful conversation—Joe had always handled my vulnerabilities with care. He had never once used them against me. Until that moment.

Hurt became fury. I said things I am not proud of and hung up.

That evening I called him. No answer. I sent a text: "I'm really, really sorry for what I said. You hit a nerve. I'm struggling with turning 45 in ways I haven't admitted out loud. I'm afraid you won't want me anymore because I'm getting older and you could find someone younger. I know I've been needy. I'm sorry. I love you."

He didn't respond. I told myself it wasn't the first time we'd gone silent for a stretch. He was under pressure. He had finally settled his custody arrangement and wanted to be fully present with his daughter during their time together. He watched my Facebook stories every day. I could see it. He was there, even when he wasn't saying anything.

In June he commented on a video of my kitten. "She's demonic." I sent a laugh emoji. The next day I texted to tell him I was bringing Gabriel to Washington D.C. in August. A school project on Abraham Lincoln had turned into a campaign from Gabe to see the monuments in person. Joe responded immediately. He wanted to see me. He wanted the kids to finally meet. He said he missed me.

The Dream

The following week was the Fourth of July. I flew to Fort Lauderdale with my parents to watch Gabriel compete at the AAU Karate National Championships. Joining the competition team had transformed him completely. He had competed at a national qualifier in May and taken silver in kumite, earning his invitation to Nationals. My business partner, an investor in Banríon, chartered a yacht one evening for the whole group. My best friend Brittany, in Florida for swim week, was there. The business was growing. Gabriel was extraordinary on the mat. Everything felt full and alive and right.

After we returned home, I had plans to look at houses. The rental we had been living in was fine for what it had needed to be, but the landlord was difficult and unresponsive about maintenance. I was ready for something that was genuinely ours. I hadn't spoken to Joe since his text about August. I'd been consumed by Nationals, then by the house search, and then by the ordinary momentum of a full life.

I went to bed early on Thursday, July 13.

The dream was vivid in a way that dreams rarely are. The doorbell rang. I dragged myself to answer it. Joe was standing on the other side, and the look on his face was something between panic and desperation. Before I could speak, he said: "I will love you forever. You will always have my heart." I closed the door. He pushed it open and said it again. I told him to leave. He kept repeating it, over and over, each time with more urgency, as if he needed me to hear something I was refusing to accept. I woke up drenched in a cold sweat. The clock read 2:30 a.m. I went to the bathroom, splashed cold water on my face, and went back to bed.

Friday was ordinary. Saturday I looked at houses.

Your Joseph

When I got home from the house tours on Saturday, there was a message request waiting in Facebook Messenger. It was from Joe's mother.

"Shana, please call me as soon as you can."

I texted Joe immediately. "Why is your mother messaging me?" His family had known we'd reconnected, but we had kept things quiet. Joe had wanted to wait until we were officially engaged before bringing our families fully into it. He knew they would never let him hear the end of how long it had taken him to find his way back to me.

He didn't respond. She messaged again. "Shana please call me as soon as you can. It's about Joseph."

I typed back: "If Joe needs something he can call me himself."

Her reply appeared on the screen and I felt the air leave the room.

"Shana. Joseph is gone."

I stopped. "Big Joseph or Little Joseph?" Joe's father was also named Joseph. He was in his late 80s. He had been having health problems. Joe had been worried about him.

Two words came back.

"YOUR JOSEPH."

I called her. She told me they had found him Friday morning. He had died in his sleep. He was 46 years old.

Forty-six. Fit. Health-conscious. No warning, no illness, no explanation that made any sense. He had simply gone to sleep and not woken up. The same night I had that dream. The clock had read 2:30 a.m.

The tears came fast and they stayed for weeks. My best friend Shawna appeared at my door within the hour—a bottle of vodka in one hand, cupcakes in the other—and sat with me through the night. The days that followed blurred together.

His family had his body flown to Florida. His father was hospitalized and unable to travel; Arlington Cemetery did not yet have a plot available. I flew to Orlando for the funeral. Our arrival gate was the same one I had watched him board a plane from just months before. His family treated me as though I were his widow. They knew what I had been to him. They knew he had planned to propose. They knew he had loved me for the better part of his entire adult life. The service was beautiful. I moved through it feeling like I was watching from somewhere slightly outside my own body.

I came home to moving boxes. I had signed a lease on a new house just days before his funeral, and the move-in date had not changed simply because the world had. As I unpacked, I noticed my back had started to ache. "This is what happens when you get old," I said to myself and didn't give it another thought.

It turned out that Joe's death was not the worst thing that would happen to me in 2023.

What Loss Teaches About the Only Investment That Cannot Be Taken

There is no market framework for grief. There is no allocation model for the loss of someone who was, in the deepest sense, the person you were always supposed to end up with. I will not pretend otherwise.

What I can do is tell you what the experience of this chapter—of Joe's death, of the years of near-misses and reconnections, and of the love story that never quite got to its final chapter—clarified for me about the things worth investing in and the things that are not.

Joe died at 46. Healthy. Intentional about his body, his career, his children, his future. He had plans. He had recently started a demanding new role. He was finishing a PhD. He was navigating custody arrangements with care. He was buying a house. He was going to propose. He had more in motion than most people half his age.

None of it was enough to give him more time.

That fact—the simple, irreducible fact of it is the most clarifying thing I have ever encountered about what actually matters and what is merely urgent:

- Time is the only truly finite asset. Capital can be rebuilt. Reputation can be restored. Careers can be restarted. Every other resource in this book—savings, credentials, professional networks, brand equity—has some mechanism of recovery or replenishment. Time does not. Joe spent years in a careful holding pattern with me—waiting for the custody situation to resolve, the divorce to finalize, the right moment to make things official. He was not careless with his love for me. He was cautious with his circumstances. And then there was no more time for the plans that were almost ready. The cost of waiting for perfect conditions is not always visible until it is too late to play it differently.
- The most important relationships in your life are not a reward for professional success—they are the context in which professional success either means something or doesn't. I had spent years treating my career as the primary investment and my personal life as something that would come together when the timing was right. What this period of my life made undeniable is that the inverse is equally true: no professional achievement produces meaning in isolation. The moments that matter—Joe watching my TV clips from Washington D.C. and asking how I was still so "smoking hot," Gabriel running across a tournament floor to tell me he wanted to join the competition team, Shawna at my door with vodka and cupcakes at the worst hour of my life—these are the returns that compound in ways no portfolio statement can capture.

- Unresolved conflict is its own form of risk. The argument with Joe in April 2023 was one of the most painful exchanges of my life, and he was dead before I had the chance to move past it with him in person. We had reconciled through text. I knew he had forgiven me. His family told me, without hesitation, how much he had loved me. But I will carry the memory of that argument alongside the memory of every good thing between us, because I did not get the opportunity to supersede it with something better. In investing, letting a position sit in a damaged state—unaddressed, unexamined, assumed to have time to recover—is how small losses become permanent ones. In relationships, the same is true. The repair you are postponing may not have the runway you are assuming it does.
- Presence is not a soft skill. It is the primary one. One of the details of this chapter that I return to most often is the urgency I felt in Orlando. The inexplicable need to tell Joe how much I loved him, to be fully there, to take the photograph, to go back for one more goodbye. I had no rational reason to feel that way. Something in me knew what my mind did not. Investing in presence—in the people, the moments, the experiences that are actually in front of you—is not a consolation prize for people who have stopped being ambitious. It is the most sophisticated allocation a person can make, because it is the one that produces returns that have no market equivalent.
- What you build inside yourself cannot be taken in the night. Joe's death stripped away, in a single phone call, a future I had been building toward for 25 years. The grief was total. What it could not touch was what had been developed through all of it: the capacity to love that completely, the willingness to be that vulnerable, the knowledge that I had been chosen by someone extraordinary even if the story didn't get

> its happy ending. Those are not small things. The inner life you build through the full accumulation of your experience—the hard years and the magical ones, the losses and the recoveries—is the only asset that is truly yours. It cannot be restructured, outsourced, or terminated with a phone call.

I came home from Joe's funeral and unpacked boxes in a house he would never see. My back ached from the lifting. I told myself it was age.

I was wrong about that too. But that is the next chapter.

What I know now that I did not know then is that the period beginning in the summer of 2023 would require every ounce of what the preceding chapters of this book had built in me. The resilience. The stubbornness. The refusal to be defined by the worst thing that is currently happening. The deep and unshakeable knowledge of my own worth that had been forged, improbably, through two decades of being tested.

The darkest chapters are not the end of the story. They are where you find out what you are actually made of. And what you do with what you find.

Chapter 20

Falling Apart: When the World Comes Crashing Down

Something Is Wrong

The back pain I had brushed off as age in early September persisted. A week later I was scheduled for Botox injections in my shoulders—a treatment I'd been using for years to manage the aftermath of a 2017 car accident that had left me with a pinched occipital nerve. Regular occipital nerve blocks helped with the nerve pain. The tight, exhausted shoulder muscles remained. Botox turned out to be the solution. It was maintenance. Routine. Something I managed the way you manage the ordinary inconveniences of a body that has been through things.

A few days after the injections I boarded a plane to Boston. I had a speaking engagement I was genuinely excited about, followed by time with my family. I packed a heating pad and a large bottle of Advil and told myself I'd handle the back situation when I got home.

When we landed, I stood up to deplane and couldn't straighten. I shuffled off the jetway hunched like I was carrying something I couldn't put down. In the cab I joked about getting old. The driver laughed. When we arrived at the hotel, I needed help getting out of the car. I stopped joking.

4 a.m., Room 412

I unpacked my heating pad, took a double dose of Advil, ordered dinner from my favorite spot in the North End, and went to bed. I couldn't get comfortable. Eventually exhaustion won.

Around 4 a.m., I woke up and could not move. I mean that precisely—not stiff, not sore, not reluctant to move. I could not move. I felt the nausea rising and had nowhere to go. I managed to roll myself off the edge of the bed and onto the floor. I pulled myself across the carpet, fistful by fistful, to the bathroom. I vomited. When I did, a bolt of pain ran the full length of my spine that I have no adequate language for. I wept on the bathroom floor. I dragged myself back to the bed, grabbed the mattress and leveraged myself up, and lay flat on my back staring at the ceiling, perfectly still, because any movement made it worse.

I couldn't reach the phone. I asked Siri to call the front desk.

The woman who answered could tell immediately that I was not describing a muscle cramp. I told her not to call 911. She heard what I sounded like and did it anyway. The paramedics arrived within minutes and could not get in. I had deadbolted the door and secured the chain before bed. It took the fire department to remove the door from its hinges. By the time they were inside I was not entirely sure what was happening to me, only that something was very wrong.

They rushed me to the emergency room, which happened to be directly next door. I don't remember the intake. I don't remember them taking my vitals. I remember waking up alone in a dimly lit room, no call button within reach, nurses moving past the doorway without stopping. I called for help until my voice gave out. Then I asked Siri to call my mom.

It was not yet 6 a.m. She picked up immediately. The hour told her everything before I said a word. "Mom. I'm at MGH. I can't move. No one is helping me. I need my mom."

She told me she'd be there as fast as she could. My parents live an hour from Boston. It was rush hour. I waited.

Ellen Orczyk Has Entered the Building

My mother is fearless and has absolutely no qualms about making a scene when a scene needs to be made. She arrived at 9:30 and did exactly that. The nurses who had been able to walk past my doorway for five-and-a-half hours found, quite suddenly, that they could not walk past my mother. A nurse appeared. Then a doctor. Someone finally brought me a glass of water.

The diagnosis: back spasms. They administered a Toradol injection, wrote me a prescription for oxycodone, and told me to get a massage. I could not walk. My mother rolled me out in a wheelchair.

The hotel found a massage therapist who could come within the hour. My mom stayed until I fell asleep. The next morning, I called the conference and told them I wouldn't be speaking. My sister Kerri arrived and then her husband Dan. Kerri went into full drill-sergeant mode, which is exactly what the situation required. She packed my things, got me dressed, and got me to the airport with wheelchair service arranged curbside. I called my friend Victoria from the gate and asked if she could meet me at O'Hare and drive my car home, because I couldn't walk and I couldn't drive. She said yes before I finished the sentence.

I got home. An hour later Jason arrived with Gabriel—he had kept him an extra few days while I was in Boston, and when I told him what had happened, he brought Gabe to me since I couldn't drive to school pickup. Gabriel came running into my room with his usual uncontainable joy, climbed up onto the bed, and declared it snuggle time. I took a muscle relaxer and some Excedrin Migraine—which turned out to be the only cocktail that actually worked—and let myself be held by my eight-year-old. The oxycodone I had flushed in Boston. Opioids and I do not get along.

Two-and-a-Half Months of Wrong Answers

My pain specialist told me the Botox could not possibly be responsible. She said back pain was frequently a manifestation of mental and emotional trauma, and given that Joe had just died, what I was experiencing was likely grief expressing itself physically. She gave me the name of a therapist who specialized in cognitive behavioral therapy for chronic pain. I knew she was wrong. I went to doctor after doctor over the next two-and-a-half months. No one had an answer.

At the end of October, I found Dr. Cha. He didn't know yet what was causing the problem, but he believed the pain was real—which, after weeks of being told it was in my head, mattered more than I can explain. He suspected the intercostal nerve and recommended a nerve block. I knew from years of occipital nerve blocks how quickly they worked when they were the right treatment. A week later I was lying face down in the procedure room. Dr. Cha had an ultrasound wand on my spine and went quiet. He finished the procedure. I waited an hour. I felt exactly the same. The nerve block had done nothing. He ordered an X-ray.

I went to the hospital the day before Gabriel and I were leaving for Boston for Thanksgiving. They would call with the results on Monday.

A Compression Fracture

I was still in constant pain when we arrived in Boston. It had become my baseline by then. I had alarms set every six hours for my Tizanidine and Excedrin. When the phone rang shortly before noon on Monday, I was not prepared.

I had a compression fracture at T7. A broken vertebra.

I couldn't understand how. You know when you break something. There is a moment, a cause, an event you can point to. I hadn't fallen. I hadn't been in an accident. How does a person fracture a vertebra and not know what happened? It made no sense, but Dr. Cha's instructions were clear: get an MRI as soon as I was back in Chicago.

Thanksgiving morning I woke up screaming. My brother Neal heard me from across the Airbnb and came running. He literally picked me up and carried me to the car. I sat at my family's Thanksgiving table barely present, in agony I had stopped being able to hide. Somehow, I got Gabriel and myself to the airport. Jason picked Gabe up that evening as planned. The following evening, I went for the MRI. When it was finished, the technician handed me the CD and told me I should go directly to the emergency room. She said I looked miserable.

She wasn't wrong, but I was not going to a hospital at 7 p.m. I'd go to orthopedic urgent care in the morning. I called my friend Shawna and asked if she could take my dog for a few days while I sorted out what was going on with my back. She was at my door 30 minutes later. She helped me get settled and ordered food before she left.

The Look on His Face

I arrived at orthopedic urgent care the next morning with my MRI CD and whatever was left of my patience. The doctor had me perform basic mobility tests. I passed them all, which surprised him. He took the CD to the radiologist. When he came back 30 minutes later, I could read the answer on his face before he sat down.

"Shana, you have a burst fracture."

There was a lesion in my spine. It had caused T7 and T8 to burst—not crack, not compress, but shatter into thousands of fragments now floating in spinal fluid. T6 was fractured as well. He didn't yet know what had caused the lesion, but I needed to see a specialist immediately. I didn't know what a lesion was. I felt too embarrassed to ask. I Googled it in the parking lot.

A lesion is a tumor.

Lytic lesions, I learned, almost always indicate cancer.

I sat in my car for a while. I had no family history of cancer. I was in the best physical shape of my life—yoga, Pilates, a personal trainer twice a week. I didn't feel sick. I felt injured. There is a difference, and I was certain I could feel it. There had to be another explanation.

He had prescribed codeine for the pain. I went home, took a Tizanidine alongside it, and went to sleep. At 3 a.m. I woke up violently ill. Opioids. I crawled to the bathroom. Projectile vomiting with a shattered spine is precisely as terrible as it sounds. I called 911. For the second time in three months I was in an ambulance.

This time I would not be going home in a few hours.

December

As soon as I was admitted, the diagnostics began. MRIs. CT scans. Every organ, every system. Nothing conclusive. I was transferred to Evanston Hospital for a bone biopsy. Shawna never left my side. Jason came by the day I was admitted to let me know he was traveling to Dubai that weekend and I would need to figure out Gabriel's care. With no other option I called my parents, and my mother booked a flight to Chicago for the following morning.

My surgeon, Dr. Nolden—one of the top spine surgeons in the Midwest, who happened to be on call the day I was admitted—wanted to wait for the biopsy results before scheduling surgery.

The results could determine which procedure was performed. So we waited.

I was never alone. My mom. Shawna. Brittany, who had flown in from Las Vegas the moment she heard. And one visitor I hadn't expected: Gabriel's sensei, John Fonseca. He came to the hospital, brought food, stayed when my mom needed a break. The dojo mobilized without being asked. Other senseis drove Gabriel to and from class. Dojo moms dropped meals at the house. Others stepped in to babysit so my mother could visit me. A community I had wandered into—through a tournament Gabe had finished dead last in—had become, without my fully realizing it, my tribe.

A full week passed with no biopsy results. Dr. Nolden decided it was no longer reasonable to wait. Surgery was scheduled for Wednesday, December 6. Whatever the lesion turned out to be, my spine needed to be repaired.

The surgery was long and complicated. When it was finished, six vertebrae had been fused. Twelve-inch metal rods and eight screws now ran from T4 to T12. I would need to learn to walk again. The recovery would be long. But the structure that had been destroying itself from the inside was finally held together.

On December 8, two days after surgery, my mother went to the Fonseca Martial Arts 20th Anniversary Celebration without me. Gabriel was receiving the Dojo Spirit Award in recognition of his impact on the other students and his dedication to the sport. I had bought a new dress and sparkly heels for the occasion. Instead, I was lying in a hospital bed, waiting.

There's No Easy Way to Say This

The biopsy results arrived that afternoon. The doctor came to my room with the head of oncology. Brittany was with me. They asked her to step out. I told them I wanted her to stay.

The doctor sat down.

"There's no easy way to say this. You have breast cancer. It is advanced stage metastatic breast cancer. The cancer has spread to your spine, and that is what caused the fractures."

I had been in that hospital for weeks. I had been in pain since September. Every scan they had run had shown nothing. And now a doctor was sitting beside my bed, two days after spinal fusion surgery, telling me I had terminal cancer. Joe had been dead for five months. Gabriel was eight years old.

I was in complete and total disbelief. The kind that doesn't feel like denial—it feels like a fundamental refusal of information that cannot possibly be true. And yet somewhere beneath the shock, beneath the noise and the fear and the sheer impossibility of the moment, something in me was already certain. I was going to live. I didn't know what that would look like or what it would cost me. I didn't know what the doctors would say next or what the road ahead contained.

But that night, lying in a hospital bed with metal rods in my spine and a diagnosis I hadn't seen coming, I looked at what was in front of me, and I made a decision. I was going to be there to watch my son grow up. I didn't need a prognosis to know that. I needed to decide it, and I did.

What I didn't have, not yet, was any idea who I was on the other side of that decision. I had built an identity over four decades out of career, ambition, resilience, and reinvention. Now I was looking at something that didn't care about any of it. The most terrifying thing about that night wasn't the diagnosis. It was the silence on the other side of it and not knowing yet what I was going to find there.

The Risk You Cannot Model

Every framework in this book—every lesson about market cycles, behavioral bias, regulatory change, portfolio construction, and the discipline required to hold conviction under pressure—was built on an implicit assumption: that the investor making the decisions is present, is functional, and has time.

Stage IV cancer is the risk that assumption never accounted for.

I am not going to wrap this chapter in a tidy investing metaphor. What happened in the fall and winter of 2023 was not a market correction I navigated skillfully or a forced reallocation that turned out better than expected. It was the most serious thing that has ever happened to me, and it happened without warning, without a signal I recognized in time, and with consequences that are still unfolding as this book goes to press.

What I can offer is what the experience has clarified—about risk, about preparation, and about the things that are actually worth protecting:

- The risks that matter most are frequently the ones that produce no signal until they are already severe. I was in the best shape of my adult life when the cancer was found. I had no family history. I felt injured, not ill, and that distinction was real, because the pain was genuinely structural. The cancer had been growing quietly, doing damage from the inside, while every external measure suggested health. This is precisely how the most dangerous risks behave in markets as well. The conditions that precede the most severe dislocations are almost never characterized by visible distress. They are characterized by stability, by strong performance, by the absence of obvious warning signs. The danger compounds in the silence. By the time the signal arrives it is already late.

- Early detection is not a luxury—it is the investment strategy. Had the lesion been identified in September rather than December, the fractures might have been avoided. The surgery might have been less extensive. The recovery would have been different. In markets, the equivalent is continuous monitoring—not obsessive daily tracking, but genuine, systematic attention to what is actually happening beneath the surface of a portfolio. The investors who avoid catastrophic losses are not always the ones with the best analysis. They are frequently the ones who looked more regularly and more honestly at what their positions were actually doing. Willingness to see what is there, rather than what you hope is there, is a discipline that applies to portfolios and to bodies with equal force.
- The infrastructure you build in good times determines your capacity in the worst ones. I did not face this diagnosis alone. I had Shawna, who never left. Brittany, who flew across the country. My mother, who booked a flight before I finished the sentence. A dojo community that mobilized without being asked. A business I owned outright that did not collapse because I was hospitalized. The investments I had made in relationships, in community, in building something portable and genuinely mine—these were not social niceties. They were structural supports that held the weight of the worst period of my life. No financial plan fully accounts for what you will need when you cannot function. The people and structures around you are part of the portfolio. They deserve the same intentional investment.
- How you respond to information you didn't want is one of the most important decisions you will ever make. The diagnosis was delivered, and I had a choice about what to do with it. Not about the cancer itself—that was not within my control.

But about the narrative I was going to build around it, the identity I was going to inhabit while I fought it, the decision I was going to make about what came next. Investors face versions of this constantly: receiving information that contradicts the thesis, learning something that invalidates the plan, confronting a reality that is worse than the model predicted. The quality of the decision made in that moment—not in the comfort of normal conditions but in the disorientation of bad news—is what separates the investors who recover from those who don't.

- The goal is not to avoid loss. It is to survive it with your capacity intact. There is no investment strategy, no level of preparation, no amount of expertise that eliminates the possibility of a catastrophic outcome. Joe understood this better than anyone I have known, and he still died at 46 in his sleep. The honest purpose of everything this book has argued for—the resilience, the brand equity, the portable expertise, the community, the financial discipline—is not to prevent the worst from happening. It is to ensure that when it does, you have something left to work with. That you are not starting from nothing at the exact moment you can afford it least. That the people and resources and inner resources you have built are available to you when you need them most.

I was lying in a hospital bed with a terminal diagnosis, metal rods in my spine, and an eight-year-old son who needed his mother to come home. I had no idea what came next. What I had was 20 years of being tested and refusing to be finished by it.

It turned out that was enough to begin.

The rest of the story is still being written.

Chapter 21

Rising from the Ashes: Embracing Life, Legacy, and Alternative Investing

Tacos and Churros for All

Nothing quite prepares you for losing a great love and receiving a terminal cancer diagnosis within six months. Before Joe's death and my hospitalization, my life and my business were thriving. After them, both were in triage—literally and figuratively.

The night the biopsy results came back, my mother and my son were a few miles away at the dojo's 20th anniversary celebration. Gabriel was being recognized for his spirit and his dedication to the sport. I could not bring myself to make that call. Some news can wait a few hours, and the joy of that evening belonged entirely to him.

The hospital staff had grown fond of me over my 16 days on the floor. I was one of the youngest patients, I smiled consistently, and my circle of visitors—my mother, Shawna, Brittany, Allison, Victoria, and John—were warm and funny in ways that seemed to change the air in whatever room they occupied. When the diagnosis was delivered on a Friday, the staff quietly relaxed the visiting hour policy just for me. Shawna had brought a full spread from my favorite Mexican restaurant. The nurses snuck in throughout the evening to join our impromptu gathering. Tacos and churros and laughter until nearly 11 p.m. They say laughter is the best medicine. I can confirm that is not a platitude.

When Shawna and Brittany finally gathered their things to leave, I told them what I knew to be true even though I had no medical basis for it yet: "I'm going to be fine. Mark my words—I'll be walking in heels by my birthday in June, and we are going to have an epic party in Las Vegas to celebrate surviving 45."

The Dark Week

I was discharged 16 days after I had been admitted. I left in a walker. Getting out of bed to use the bathroom required help. The first week home was the hardest stretch of the entire ordeal—not because of the physical pain, which was considerable, but because of the silence inside it. The hospital had been relentless with stimulation: lights, beeping, vital checks, blood draws at hours that made sleep impossible. Home was quiet. Quiet gave me nowhere to put everything I was trying to process.

Banríon was in crisis. My team had held the operation together with remarkable competence during my absence, but many of our clients had come to us because of a personal relationship with me. When word spread that I was hospitalized—before the diagnosis was known, before I had any clarity to offer—a significant portion of them paused payments. Twelve months of runway began evaporating faster than any projection had anticipated. We took on debt to fill the gap until I could return to work. We had no other option.

I spent those early days at home searching for meaning in the sequence of events that had produced this moment. Joe. The back pain dismissed as grief. The wrong diagnoses. The fractures. The surgery. The words *advanced-stage metastatic breast cancer*. I also spent them terrified in ways I had not yet admitted to anyone. I had built an identity around the intersection of intellect and image. The Queen of Alternatives was not a brand that existed despite how she looked—it was one that was partly constituted by it. What happened if my hair fell out? What if treatment pushed me into medical menopause and changed my body in ways that were visible and irreversible? Would clients and prospects interpret my illness as existential risk to the firm? Who would want to build a life with a woman carrying this diagnosis? And how would Gabriel—eight years old, sharp, emotionally perceptive in the way children are when they are paying close attention—understand and survive watching his mother go through this?

My ex-husband made clear that the custody arrangement would not change. My health was my problem to manage, and I needed to ensure Gabriel had appropriate care during my time. He was right that the logistics were my responsibility. But receiving that message from a hospital bed, when I could not yet walk to the bathroom alone, was its own particular kind of hard.

My mother stayed until just before Christmas. Shawna and Brittany took over from there—Brittany moving into the guest room for the next eight weeks. They fed me, bathed me, dressed me, and tolerated my grumpiness and controlling tendencies with a grace I will never be able to adequately repay. They kept an eight-year-old entertained and emotionally regulated through something no child should have to navigate—Gabriel had become obsessed with death, telling anyone who would listen that he wanted everyone else to die if it meant his mom could live. The holidays came and went without my family for the first time in my life. My Banríon team brought Christmas to me—Victoria and her mother arrived with their entire Christmas feast and shared traditions that had nothing to do with my family's and everything to do with what I needed that day.

Still Fabulous

Once I began to accept that my life was genuinely and permanently different, I had to decide who I was going to be inside that difference.

Facing mortality does something to the architecture of anxiety. The things I had spent years worrying about—the career reversals, the financial instability, the relationships that didn't work, the image I maintained with such deliberate effort—reorganized themselves in the presence of a larger and more absolute uncertainty. If I didn't know whether I would be here in a month, in a year, in five years, what did it mean to spend the time I did have in fear of smaller losses? My previously anxious self did not gradually dissolve. It disappeared almost overnight. Whatever life was going to throw at me, it would mean I was still alive to receive it. That realization changed everything about how I moved through each day.

There is a difference between being alive and living. I made a decision that I was not going to let the illness change the essence of who I was.

The owner of my lash studio called to let me know she had paused my membership during active treatment. I told her I had no intention of giving up my beauty routine because I had become a cancer patient. I would be in for my next appointment as usual. In-home spa treatments became a staple of my recovery. Manicures continued. Brittany and I spent evenings watching Hallmark Christmas movies in collagen face masks under red light therapy. Whatever the day had taken, this was the part we kept.

When I began radiation, I made a decision about the energy I wanted to bring to the cancer center, which always carried the weight of its own particular sadness. I spent $150 on a purple rhinestone cane. I arrived at every appointment in full makeup, crop tops, leggings, knee-high boots, oversized fur coats, and at least 20 pairs of Blue Q socks with increasingly audacious slogans printed on them. "I Identify as Badass." "Turns Out I Am the Shit." "Please, One Shit Show at a Time." The radiation technicians began looking forward to the daily sock reveal. It became a ritual.

One morning I walked into the waiting room in all of it—tight black leggings, cropped turtleneck, enormous faux fur coat, full glam, dark sunglasses—and an older woman in the corner was crying. She looked up and the tears stopped. She stared for a moment. Then she smiled. "Well, you are just a whole vibe, aren't you?"

I laughed. "I have cancer, but I'm still fabulous."

The next day I saw her, and she shared with me that the previous day she had gone home and insisted her husband take her on a date night in the city. They both got dressed up. She said it was the first time since her diagnosis that she had, for a few hours, completely forgotten she was sick. When I walked in that morning and changed the energy of that waiting room, it reminded her that she wasn't dead yet. That there was a way to move through this that did not require surrendering yourself to it.

I had already known, in the abstract, that how you carry yourself through difficulty affects everyone around you. In that waiting room, I understood it in a different way. The choice to remain fully yourself—to refuse to become only a patient, only a diagnosis, only a set of limitations—is not vanity, and it is not denial. It is an act of defiance that has a gravitational pull. Other people feel it and are changed by it.

The Red Lipstick

I kept the details of my diagnosis within a small circle for much of my treatment. I was not hiding. I was protecting the energy around my recovery and being deliberate about the key-woman risk perception at Banríon. I had built the firm around my identity and my presence. If clients and prospects knew the full picture before I had proof of my own recovery to offer alongside it, fear might do damage that the illness itself had not.

But I gave the world one quiet signal. For every media appearance and every stage I stood on during active treatment, I wore blood red lipstick. Deliberately. Jarringly. It was a declaration dressed as an aesthetic choice, visible to anyone paying attention, invisible to anyone who wasn't.

Active treatment was not easy. The radiation compromised my esophagus severely—there were weeks when swallowing my own saliva was excruciating. I lost significant weight. At my lowest I weighed 92 pounds. Learning to walk without assistance, and eventually to wear heels again for any real length of time, took approximately 15 months—far longer than the declaration I had made in the hospital that night had accounted for.

But the declaration held. June arrived. I was in Las Vegas. I was in heels. We celebrated. See Figure 21.1.

What Remains

My career and my business took a substantial hit. Financial stability is still something I am rebuilding rather than inhabiting. My dating life is essentially nonexistent. The simple, comfortable dream I described at the start of this chapter—the modest house, the love, the reliable ordinary life my parents had—remains unfinished.

I am alive. I am living. I am more present than I have ever been in my life. I am a better investor. I am better equipped to handle whatever comes next than I have ever been, not despite everything that happened but because of it.

By March I was using the cane only occasionally. By April not at all. By May I had achieved remission. By June I was in Las Vegas in heels, celebrating being 46 and alive and still, unmistakably, myself.

That is not a small thing. It is, in fact, the whole thing.

Figure 21.1 I had cancer, but I'm still fabulous!

Your Turn: One Last Look Back Before You Move Forward

Before you close this book, go back. Find every "Your Turn" you encountered across these chapters—the questions about your upbringing and your relationship with money, your instincts under pressure, your fears, your drive, the advice that changed your direction, the hardship that built something in you that comfort

(continued)

(continued)

never could have. Read what you wrote, or what you thought but never put down. Then choose one. Not the easiest one, the one that, if you acted on it, would change something real. The one you have been circling without fully committing to. Every chapter of this book has argued that your life has already been preparing you for this. The "Your Turns" were not exercises. They were an inventory of your actual edge: the self-knowledge, the hard-won clarity, the specific and irreplaceable understanding of risk and resilience that only comes from having lived what you have lived. That inventory is useful only if you do something with it. You do not need to act on all of it at once. You need to act on one thing, with intention, and let that compound into the next. That is how it works in markets. That is how it works in life. You have everything you need. You always did. Now use it.

You Already Are

Most of you came to this book to become a better investor. I want to tell you something that I hope the preceding 20 chapters have been building toward quietly, and that I am now ready to say directly: you already are one.

Not because you finished the book. Not because of anything I have taught you about alternatives or regulatory change or the behavioral patterns that drive markets or the discipline required to hold conviction when everyone around you is capitulating. Those things matter. They are worth knowing. But they are not the source of the insight that makes a truly good investor.

The source is everything that happened to you before you opened this book.

The challenges that shaped how you think about risk. The losses that taught you what you actually value. The moments of forced clarity—the job you didn't get, the relationship that ended badly, the diagnosis you didn't see coming, the season when nothing worked and you had to decide whether you were finished or just interrupted. The communities that caught you when institutions failed. The times you were right and ignored, and the times you were wrong and had to admit it. The version of yourself that showed up on the other side of every single one of those things.

That is the investor. That is the raw material no credential can manufacture and no textbook can produce.

Here is what this book has really been arguing, from the first chapter to this one:

- Your lived experience is your most valuable source of market intelligence. The investors who build lasting insight are not the ones who spend the most time at a desk. They are the ones who pay attention to the world they are actually living in—to where systems are straining before they break, to what people are adopting before it becomes a trend, to the regulatory shifts that are happening quietly while the headlines point elsewhere. Your life has been preparing you to see those things. You only need to start trusting what you already notice.
- Resilience is not a personality trait. It is a repeatable skill. Every chapter of this book described a version of the same fundamental process: something breaks, a decision is made about what to do next, and the decision made in that moment—not in the comfort of stable conditions but in the disorientation of loss—determines everything that follows. That process can be developed, refined, and deliberately applied. The investors who build lasting wealth are not the ones who avoided

hard years. They are the ones who treated hard years as the education they were.

- Conviction without independence is not conviction. It is compliance. The moments in this book when the right call was dismissed—the Apple pitch, the market bottom in March 2009, the early case for alternatives when hedge funds were being blamed for the crisis—were not moments of bad luck. They were reminders that the market, the committee, and the consensus are frequently wrong at the exact moment it is most expensive to agree with them. Building the credibility to act on your own analysis, in the face of institutional pressure or social disapproval, is one of the most important things you can invest in. It takes years. It is worth every one of them.
- The assets that compound most reliably are the ones no one can take from you. Brand. Expertise. Genuine relationships. Community. The inner architecture of a person who has been tested and has not been finished by it. These do not appear on a balance sheet. They are not marked to market. They cannot be restructured in a deal or terminated with a phone call. And they are, in the final accounting, the only things that were still fully intact every single time the external structures around me collapsed. Build them first. Build them always.
- The goal was never to avoid the difficult things. It was to become someone who could move through them. I did not set out to lose four jobs in two years, to grieve the love of my life and receive a terminal diagnosis in the same season, to launch a firm from an empty bank account with a Disney trip to fund somehow. None of that was the plan. All of it shaped the investor, the founder, and the person I am today in ways that no amount of planning could have produced. The willingness to remain in the game—to keep showing up, to keep paying

attention, to keep building even when the outcome is uncertain and the conditions are genuinely hard—is the most important edge any investor can develop. It does not come from optimism. It comes from having survived enough to know that survival is possible.

I began this book with a story about where I came from—the immigrant mindset, the blue-collar values, the people who shaped how I understood work and risk and what it meant to earn something. I am ending it in a hospital bed with metal rods in my spine, a company held together by people who believed in what we were building, a son who wanted to give everyone else in the world his extra years if it meant his mother could keep hers, and the absolute, unshakeable certainty that I was not done.

That certainty did not come from a credential or a market call or a perfectly timed exit. It came from 20 years of choosing, again and again, to remain in the game.

Alternative investments changed how I saw markets. But it was my life that changed how I saw everything else. And it turns out—as I hope this book has made clear—those two things were never as separate as they seemed.

You already have everything you need to be a great investor. You always did. Pay attention to your life. Trust what you know. Do the work. Stay in the game.

The rest will compound.

Epilogue

I always wanted to write a book because I believed my story was worth telling. A year ago, a message from an editor at Wiley made that possibility a reality. I signed on with a firm belief that I was moving toward a happy ending—one that would show others that hardship, accumulated and endured, ultimately leads somewhere better. This is a testament to the idea that the arc of a difficult life bends, eventually, toward something worth having.

The arc is still bending.

As I write this, it has been nearly three years since Joe died and my world came apart in the span of a single season. The events of 2023 did not just test me. They remade me in ways I am still in the process of understanding. Before July of that year, I was certain that Banríon's immediate success and the speed of my professional turnaround were signs that I had finally found the path. The firm was going to be the proof. It was proof for Gabriel of what his mother was capable of, proof for me that the modest, full, love-rich life I had been working toward since childhood was finally within reach.

The reality is more complicated and more honest than that.

A cancer diagnosis does something particular to a founder's ability to raise capital. Investors don't write checks to people they aren't confident will be there to execute the vision. They don't write checks to women navigating chemotherapy and motherhood without a support structure at home, regardless of track record or conviction or the clarity of the idea. No amount of grinding, no volume of press coverage, and no number of conference stages can fully override the perception that a founder is stretched beyond what the moment requires. I know what I am capable of. I know what I have built and what I have survived. But knowing your own worth and being able to convince the gatekeepers of capital are not always the same thing, and a business cannot be sustained on vision alone. The debt that carried us through the hardest months eventually comes due.

There is no great love waiting for me at home at the end of a difficult day. Not yet. The simple, quiet life I have been dreaming about since I was a little girl watching my parents build something solid together—the house, the love, the ordinary Tuesday evening that feels like enough—remains unfinished. I say that not to solicit pity. I say it because this book was written in the spirit of honesty, and the honest ending of this particular chapter is that the story is still being written.

What I have learned, through everything this book contains, is that the most important things in a life are not things. That is not an original observation, and I am aware of how it sounds. But there is a difference between knowing something and having it proven to you, repeatedly, at cost. I know it now in my body, in my bones, in the part of me that was remade by the losses that did not finish me.

In the darkest moments I have ever lived through, people showed up. Brittany flew across the country without being asked. Shawna never left. John Fonseca—a man I met because my seven-year-old finished last at a karate tournament and couldn't stop crying—brought food to a hospital room and sat with a woman he barely knew because it was the right thing to do. My family. My Banríon team, who held everything together while I lay in a hospital bed unable to walk. The Fonseca martial arts (FMA) community, who rallied around Gabriel and around me with a consistency and a warmth I did not know I was missing until I found it. I found my tribe in the most unexpected places, at the bottom of the hardest years, and I am more grateful for them than I have words for.

The financial markets I fell in love with 25 years ago continue to ignite something in me that nothing else does. Not for the money. Money has come and gone and come again, and I have stopped treating its presence or absence as a measure of anything fundamental. But because those markets are endlessly alive with the questions I love most: why do people value what they value, what does the world believe about the future, and where is the gap between what everyone thinks they know and what is actually true? That passion, sustained over decades of being underestimated and overcoming and starting over, is what earned me the title of Queen of Alternatives. And whatever comes next, no one can take that from me.

I wouldn't change a single thing about this life. Not the losses, not the wrong turns, not the years that felt like they were breaking me. Without all of it, I wouldn't have this story. And without this story, I couldn't offer you the thing I most want to leave you with.

So many people look at financial markets and feel immediately overwhelmed. The numbers, the jargon, the credentialed professionals who speak in a language designed to remind you that you don't belong—it is intimidating by design. But here is what 25 years inside those markets has taught me and what every chapter of this book has been quietly arguing: markets are not a mathematical abstraction. They are a collective human opinion about value. They are shaped by fear and hope and grief and ambition and the same forces that have shaped every story in this book. They are shaped by people. And you have been a student of people your entire life.

You already know how to read a room. You already know when something is overvalued by the enthusiasm surrounding it and when something real is being ignored. You already know what it costs to hold a position when everyone around you is telling you to let it go and what it feels like to be right about something that takes too long to prove. You already know that the most important decisions are made not in conditions of certainty but in conditions of genuine fear and that the quality of those decisions is what separates the people who build something lasting from the people who participate only when it's comfortable.

You learned all of that from your life. Not from a textbook. Not from a credential. From the specific, irreplaceable, unrepeatable accumulation of everything that has happened to you.

That is the investor. That is where the edge lives.

Don't stop asking questions. Don't stop observing. Don't stop learning from the world that is actually moving around you, the one you are already inside of, the one that has been teaching you all along.

True wealth is not built in the balance of a bank account. It is built in the richness of the life you create along the way—in the people you find, the purpose you discover, the version of yourself that emerges from the years that tried to break you and didn't.

That is what it means to be tough minded.

Now go build something.

Glossary

130/30 and 120/20 mutual funds: Mutual funds that use a modest amount of leverage and short selling, strategies previously available only in hedge funds, within a regulated, accessible fund structure. A 130/30 fund, for example, takes $130 worth of long positions for every $100 invested by borrowing against $30 worth of short positions it has simultaneously placed against stocks it expects to decline. The net exposure remains 100%; it is not a reckless bet, but the structure allows the manager to express both positive and negative views on individual securities, potentially generating better returns than a traditional long-only fund. The 2007 regulatory changes to the Investment Company Act made these structures available in registered mutual funds for the first time, opening a door that had previously been reserved for institutional investors only.

529 plan: A tax-advantaged savings account specifically designed to help families save for education expenses. The name comes from the section of the tax code that created it, but the concept is straightforward: you contribute money to the account, it grows tax-free, and as long as the funds are used for qualified education expenses, tuition, room and board, books, and in many cases K-12 education and vocational programs, you never pay taxes on the growth. Many states also offer a tax deduction on contributions, making the benefit even more valuable.

Alternative investments: Any investment that falls outside the three traditional asset classes of publicly traded stocks, bonds, and cash. However, the category is broader and more varied than most people realize. Some alternatives, like hedge funds, managed futures, and commodities, offer exposure to strategies and assets that behave very differently from public markets, providing genuine diversification when stocks and bonds decline together. Others, like private equity and private credit, invest in fundamentally similar things to their public counterparts—companies and loans—but do so through private, less regulated structures that are not traded on public exchanges. The distinction matters: private equity and private credit don't necessarily zig when public markets zag, but they offer different return profiles, liquidity terms, and access to opportunities that simply don't exist in public markets. What unites the category is that alternative investments have historically required large minimum investments and been available only to institutions and wealthy individuals who qualified as accredited investors. That has been changing steadily, driven by regulatory shifts that have created new vehicles bringing these strategies within reach of a much broader population. The core appeal varies by strategy, some alternatives add genuine diversification, others add return potential or income, and others provide access to high-quality private companies and credit opportunities that public market investors simply cannot reach. Understanding which type you are using, and why, is the beginning of using them well.

Asymmetric risk: When the reward of being right is significantly larger than the cost if you're wrong. A small bet with a big potential payoff. That imbalance—between what you stand to gain and what you stand to lose—is the foundation of every great investment decision.

Bull and bear: The bull as a symbol for rising markets comes from the way the animal fights; a bull attacks by thrusting its horns upward, a motion that mirrors the upward movement of rising prices. The bear, by contrast, attacks by swiping its paws downward, which mirrors falling prices. The two animals became the enduring shorthand for the two dominant moods of financial markets—optimism and pessimism, expansion and contraction—and the imagery has stuck for centuries. A person is called a bull if they invest based on the belief that the market will go up. A person is called a bear if they invest based on the belief the market will go down.

Consensus risk: The danger of being wrong alongside everyone else at the same time. When a belief becomes widely shared, markets price it in, and when that belief turns out to be wrong, everyone rushes for the exit at once. The more comfortable and obvious a position feels, the more dangerous it often is.

Conviction investing: The practice of building a position based on your own analysis and holding it through the discomfort of being questioned or temporarily wrong because you believe the market hasn't caught up to what you already see. It is not stubbornness. Stubbornness ignores new evidence. Conviction is tested against it continuously and holds only as long as the underlying analysis still stands.

Emerging markets: Countries whose economies are growing and developing rapidly but have not yet reached the level of stability, infrastructure, or regulatory maturity of fully developed economies like the United States or Western Europe. Think of places like Brazil, India, China, Mexico, and Southeast Asian nations—economies with expanding middle classes, increasing industrial output, and significant growth potential, but also higher levels of political risk, currency volatility, and less established financial systems. For investors, emerging markets can offer the appeal of faster growth than mature economies, but they come with a higher degree of uncertainty and the understanding that the rules of the game can change more quickly and unpredictably than in more established markets.

Fannie Mae/Freddie Mac: The government-sponsored enterprises created by Congress to provide liquidity, stability, and affordability to the U.S. mortgage market. They purchase loans from lenders, free up capital for more lending, and package them into mortgage-backed securities.

FINRA securities licenses: FINRA stands for the Financial Industry Regulatory Authority. It is the organization that oversees and licenses the professionals who work in the U.S. securities industry. Earning a FINRA license requires passing a rigorous exam and demonstrates that a financial professional has met a defined standard of knowledge in their area of practice. The most common licenses referenced in this book are the Series 7, Series 66, and Series 31. Prior to 2007, the agency was called NASD, which stood for the National Association of Securities Dealers. *See also* Series 7, Series 66, and Series 31.

Hedge fund: A private investment pool that uses a wide range of strategies, including borrowing money to amplify returns, betting that prices will fall, and investing in complex instruments to generate returns regardless of whether markets are going up or down. Unlike mutual funds, hedge funds are largely unregulated and available only to wealthy individuals and institutions, which gives them the freedom to take risks and pursue strategies that traditional investment vehicles cannot.

Imposing gates: When a fund (typically a hedge fund or other private fund) has temporarily suspended or limited investors' ability to withdraw their money, essentially locking them in. The term comes from the image of a gate being closed. Funds impose gates when too many investors try to withdraw at the same time, creating a situation where the fund would be forced to sell assets too quickly and at unfavorable prices to meet those demands. While gates are written into most hedge fund agreements as a protective mechanism, having them imposed is almost always a sign of serious stress, both for the fund itself and for the broader market conditions that triggered the rush for the exits in the first place.

Leveraged buyout (LBO): When a person or firm acquires a company using mostly borrowed money rather than their own cash, similar in concept to buying a house with a mortgage, except the loan is secured against the company being purchased rather than the buyer's personal assets. The acquired company's own future earnings and assets are then used to pay back the debt over time. Private equity firms use this strategy frequently because it allows them to control a large asset with a relatively small upfront investment of their own capital. The risk is that if the company doesn't generate enough cash to service the debt, the consequences can be severe, but when it works, the returns on that small initial investment can be substantial.

Margin call: Happens when an investor has borrowed money to fund their investments and those investments have lost enough value that the lender demands they either deposit more cash or sell some assets immediately to cover the shortfall. Think of it like a bank calling in part of a loan because the collateral backing it has declined in value. Margin calls are particularly dangerous during market downturns because they force investors to sell at exactly the wrong moment, locking in losses and frequently pushing prices down further as more and more forced sellers hit the market at the same time.

Master limited partnerships (MLPs): Publicly traded companies, most commonly in the energy sector, that own and operate infrastructure like pipelines, storage facilities, and processing plants. They are structured as partnerships rather than corporations, which means they pass the majority of their cash flows directly to investors without being taxed at the corporate level first, similar to how a landlord collects rent and passes it along. This structure makes them attractive for income-seeking investors. The trade-off is that they can be less liquid than ordinary stocks, meaning they are harder to sell quickly in large quantities, which is why forced selling of MLPs during the financial crisis contributed to sudden and severe price drops that had nothing to do with the underlying businesses.

Risk concentration: What happens when too much of your money is riding on a single bet: one stock, one sector, one outcome. If that one thing goes wrong, the damage isn't contained; it's catastrophic.

Series 7 General Securities Representative License: The Series 7 is the foundational license for anyone who wants to buy and sell securities on behalf of clients. It covers a broad range of investment products—stocks, bonds, mutual funds, options, and more and is essentially the entry point into the profession of financial advising and brokerage. Passing the Series 7 is one of the first major milestones for anyone building a career in the investment industry. *See also* FINRA securities licenses.

Series 31 Futures Managed Funds Examination: The Series 31 is a more specialized license that qualifies a professional to sell managed futures funds, investment vehicles that trade futures contracts on commodities, currencies, interest rates, and other instruments. It is far less common than the Series 7 or 66 and signals a level of specialization in the alternative investment space, which is precisely why it was a natural credential to pursue given the direction my career was taking. *See also* FINRA securities licenses.

Series 66 Uniform Combined State Law Examination: The Series 66 is typically taken alongside the Series 7 and allows a financial professional to act as both a securities agent and an investment adviser representative. In practical terms, it is what permits an advisor to charge fees for investment advice rather than earning commissions only on transactions. It also covers the state-level regulations that govern how financial professionals must conduct themselves with clients. *See also* FINRA securities licenses.

Swaps desk: The team at a financial institution that trades swap contracts, agreements between two parties to exchange one stream of payments for another, most commonly trading a fixed interest rate for a floating one. Think of it as a specialized trading operation where sophisticated clients can essentially swap the financial terms of their existing obligations for ones that better suit their needs.

Tech bubble: A period in the late 1990s when investor excitement about the Internet drove technology stock prices to absurd levels completely disconnected from actual business fundamentals. When reality caught up, the market collapsed between 2000 and 2002, wiping out trillions in value almost overnight.

Turnkey asset management programs (TAMPs): Programs that provide financial advisers, broker-dealers, and other professionals with an efficient platform to manage client investment accounts. By utilizing these fee-based services, advisors save time on asset management tasks such as investment research and portfolio allocation, allowing them to concentrate on delivering expert service and attracting new clients. This delegation not only supports profitability but also offers comprehensive account management, including billing and reporting.

Index